STOCK MARKET INVESTING FOR TEENS

A GUIDE TO BUILDING KNOWLEDGE, CONFIDENCE, AND FINANCIAL FREEDOM THROUGH THE ART OF INVESTING

MYLES WEST

CONTENTS

INTRODUCTION

We cannot even begin to count the number of young adults who have seen a TV show about entrepreneurship or read a magazine article stating that they, too, can become wealthy by investing properly in stocks.

Trading in whatever type of stock is a fantastic means of obtaining income and building a solid financial foundation. Because the skills and routines you build as a youngster will last a lifetime, it is indeed vital to get started as early as possible.

I wrote this book because investing has always sparked my interest (and continues to do so), not to forget the monetary advantages. You can invest irrespective of age or financial situation, and I believe that this book will help you do so productively.

This book is meant to assist you in making money in the stock market with the ultimate aim of gaining financial freedom for its readers. Throughout the sections, you will discover how to make as well as save money (with the goal of investing it), how to open an actual account to begin trading, as well as how to understand all of the terminology, charts, and numbers that come with stocks.

You will also learn from some of history's most professional traders and see examples of real-world transactions that illustrate the concepts discussed in this book. Most people your age have not been subjected to this type of content, so be alert. It deserves to be treated with care and you should be aware of its value. Most importantly, make excellent use of it. It is incredibly potent, and if you put in the time and effort, it has the potential to dramatically change your life completely.

Early investment has numerous advantages. You can get started far sooner than if you wait until you are 20 to begin saving, which will cause a lot of 401(k) money to be locked up until retirement. You will be able to choose between a variety of investments with varying investment returns to see which ones are the perfect fit for your needs. You will also be able to get a jump start on the years ahead with your income.

There are plenty of strong reasons to begin investing now, not the least of which is the stock market's historically high yearly return of 7 percent. Other considerations come into the equation if you wait till you are older. You will have much more time to ride out all the highs and lows and overcome your concerns of the uncertainty if you begin now.

Also, because your personal economy is not as well-built as an aged investor's, it is simpler to recuperate from financial blunders when you are young. You can even save money without having to cut back on other areas of your budget. You may be able to get a jump start on your retirement and education savings if you start saving while still in high school.

Another advantage of investing young is that your gains will compound at rates that would be hard to achieve if you waited until later on in life. Except for in the case of stocks, it is similar to compound interest in the capital invested to earn interest on top of interest. So, if you invest $5,000 when you are 20, it will be worth around $131,000 when you are 65 (an 8 percent return is assumed).

Regrettably, the vast majority of young people do not invest. According to various financial reports from 2021, only 16 percent of teenagers (age 11-17) have invested in equities or stock mutual funds. However, older individuals aged 30 and above make up only 18 percent of the population.

Worse, the great majority of youngsters do not ever create a savings account or invest in anything during that portion of their life. Only 35 percent of 12 to 19-year-olds have ever established a savings account, and only 7 percent have ever engaged in stocks or stock mutual funds, according to a UBS/Gallup study.

It is, however, not too late to begin saving for retirement once you reach your twenties. According to Kirk Chisholm of Chisholm Financial Group LLC in McLean, Virginia, "There are a variety of reasons why young people are not investing in the stock market... Some people are terrified of losing money, others are unsure how much they need to save to achieve a given goal, and still, others are unsure whether investment vehicles are the finest."

This book has been put together to assist you in learning the fundamentals of the stock market. By the end of this book, you should have a good understanding of the stock market and what it entails.

1

WHY YOU SHOULD START INVESTING YOUNG

I n Canada, there is a growing trend of retired persons in their 70s and 80s returning to work. Some people do it because they enjoy working and don't want to stop. Others, on the other hand, do it because they have no choice – they just cannot afford not to. It's a sobering reality, yet many Canadians are having difficulty saving enough money for retirement.

According to recent research conducted by the accounting company, BDO Canada Limited, 39 percent of Canadians have no retirement savings, increasing the temptation to work longer. Worse, 69 percent of Canadians believe they will not have enough money to live comfortably in retirement.

It's why I began investing at a young age, so I would not have to worry about working later in life. In this book, I'll explain why you should start investing early and provide tips on how to get started so you may enjoy your golden years with peace of mind.

SEVEN REASONS TO START INVESTING AS SOON AS POSSIBLE

While it's never too late to start investing or thinking about your financial future, discover why investing in your twenties is significantly more profitable than you may believe.

1. To Put Time On Your Side

When it comes to accumulating wealth, time is your most valuable asset. The sooner you begin investing, the more time your funds have to compound and grow. Interest is similar to a snowball rolling down a hill in that it grows more and more over time. Instead of investing large sums of money over a short period of time, you can save small amounts of money and attain your goal by allowing your money to grow slowly (and significantly) over decades. The power of compound interest is responsible for this (more on this later).

If you're worried that you've waited too long, there's good news: you can begin investing right now. No matter where you are in life, it is never too late to begin investing. The first stage is to create a financial plan that outlines a strategy for achieving your retirement savings goal by a certain age. You'll need to have a specific, tangible plan in place to make up for lost time this way.

2. To Combat Inflation

Inflation is defined as a gradual increase in the price of goods and services over time. Inflation will destroy the value of a country's currency over time and is influenced by a variety of causes.

Individuals may have to stretch a fixed wage even further in order to afford increased prices each year due to inflation. It's why some companies offer a 1 to 2 percent "cost of living" compensation raise to their staff every year. Investors, on the other hand, may find that combating inflation means continuing to see returns by adding to their retirement fund.

Stocks, in most situations, have a good chance of keeping up with inflation. You must keep in mind, however, that not all stocks are made equal. During bouts of inflation, for example, high-paying dividend stocks are frequently pummeled. Fixed-rate bonds are an example of this. You should concentrate your efforts on organizations that can successfully pass on their rising costs to their potential clients. Companies in the consumer staples category (products that are necessary for everyday living, like food) are an illustration of this.

To counteract inflation, the simple line is that you should start investing early and regularly. The value of our money decreases when the cost of products and services rises. Keeping your portfolio well-diversified will help you remain ahead of the curve.

A movie ticket, for example, cost $2.89 on average in 1980. In comparison, the average cost of a movie ticket in 2019 has climbed to $9.16. If you saved a $10 bill from 1980, you'd be able to buy two fewer cinema tickets in 2019 than you could nearly four decades ago, and this trend is only expected to continue.

Though it's inconvenient to think about your money depreciating, most economists believe a modest amount of inflation to be a sign of a healthy economy. A modest rate of inflation encourages you to spend or invest your money today rather than burying it under your mattress and watching it depreciate in value.

On the other hand, inflation might be a harmful factor in an economy if it is allowed to spiral out of control. Unchecked inflation may bring a country's economy crashing down, as it did in 2018, when Venezuela's inflation rate soared to over 1,000,000 percent each month, leading the economy to collapse and prompting tens of thousands of people to escape the country.

3. You Can Take More Risks Early On

You can afford to take calculated chances in promising projects when you are young. You can't afford to take this risk as you approach retirement since you won't be able to replace your savings and lost time in compounding interest.

Thus, you may be able to afford a more aggressive portfolio when you're younger. If you are approaching retirement, on the other hand, you may need to choose a more conservative portfolio, which means your chances of seeing significant returns are minimal.

Someone who invests conservatively is attempting to safeguard their capital (their existing funds) and makes this their priority instead of growing their profits. This investor frequently maintains a low-risk tolerance. Simply put, these people are willing to forego possibly higher returns in exchange for more consistent returns. As a result, they recognize that they are unlikely to be concerned or reactive in the face of market declines.

An ultra-conservative investor might put all of their money into a bond portfolio. If they're moderately conservative, an 80/20 or 70/30 bond-to-stock ratio might be appropriate. While this is excellent for avoiding danger, it will not allow you to maximize profits.

An aggressive investor, on the other hand, is someone who isn't afraid to take risks or is still young enough to ride out the market's ups and downs. They understand that their portfolio should balance out over time, allowing them to maximize gains. An aggressive strategy would be entirely made up of equities (100 percent) or a 90/10 mix of stocks and bonds.

Alternatively, you might take a more balanced strategy and split your investments 60/40 (bonds/stocks or stocks/bonds).

However, if you're investing early, I recommend taking a more aggressive approach to maximize returns and make the most of your investment time.

Fortunately, thanks to the rise of robotic advisors (called robo-advisors), it's now easier than ever to design a diverse, well-balanced portfolio that fits your needs. A robo-advisor can assist you in constructing a portfolio that is appropriate for your risk tolerance. A robo-advisor like Wealthsimple will design a portfolio of low-cost ETFs based on your age, financial goals, and risk tolerance after you answer a few simple questions regarding these things.

4. It Allows You to Chart Your Future

Early investing gives you complete control over your financial future. You will have more flexibility to construct a financial plan, build a budget, and choose investments that are higher risk, but offer higher rewards if you start investing early.

If you begin early, you will have a lot of freedom. This is because as the time to retirement gets shorter, you will need to make wise financial decisions, save more, and live on a smaller budget. To achieve your financial objectives, you may need to invest more actively.

As a result, investing early provides you more control over your financial future, which is accomplished through the beauty of how your investments ebb and flow over time. As I previously stated, equities will rise and fall over time, but as history has demonstrated, we can attain the best long-term returns by diversifying our portfolio.

By investing ahead, you may avoid the stress of market swings and instead concentrate on creating a financial strategy for your future. Since I began investing in my teens, one of the things I've appreciated is the ability to pick stocks and try out a few concepts, as well as taking a few chances. Keep in mind that it is best to begin investing early in order to reap the benefits later in life.

You can do this without paying a lot of money if you discover a decent discount brokerage service. You can experiment with different stocks to see what works best for you by using an online broker that doesn't charge a lot of fees.

5. Investing In Your Twenties (or Any Age) Has Never Been This Easy

As previously stated, it has never been easier to begin investing early. The days of going to a physical branch, meeting with a financial counselor, and having them design your financial destiny for you are long gone. You can still do it, but it will cost you more money and provide you less control. It's for this reason that many individuals are ditching their financial advisors in favor of robo-advisors.

There is no excuse not to start investing now, especially with the development of AI-powered robo-advisors like Wealthsimple. Even if you have no idea what you're doing, a robo-advisor can rapidly and efficiently guide your finances (and at a very low cost). Many robo-advisors build out their portfolios using low-cost index funds. This is beneficial because, on average, these funds outperform actively managed funds by 80 to 90 percent.

In fact, Richard Ferri, CFA, Founder of Portfolio Solutions, and Alex Benke, CFP, Product Manager at Betterment, conducted research into the performance of index fund portfolios versus actively managed funds. The findings were incredible: they discovered that diversified index funds won 82.9 percent of the time when compared to actively managed funds. In July of 2013, the duo published their findings in the *Journal of Indexes*.

If you want to do your own investing, though, you can sign up for a low-cost online brokerage like Questrade. Questrade is a well-known favorite online brokerage for investing since it offers free ETF purchases and a wealth of free research resources. In addition, when Young and Thrifty readers sign up for Questrade, they will receive some amount of free trades. You'll be able to put a considerable amount of money into your retirement savings as a result of this.

Thus, you will save a lot of money whether you use a robo-advisor or an online brokerage for a more self-guided approach (versus paying a financial advisor). In a matter of minutes, you can sign up for Wealthsimple or Questrade and begin developing a portfolio that meets your needs.

6. To Benefit From the Magic of Compound Interest

Time isn't enough to make you wealthy. It doesn't matter how long you save if you put cash beneath your mattress; your piggy bank's money loses value over time because it can't keep up with inflation. Compound interest kicks in at this point.

Let's assume that Person A starts saving $300 per month at the age of 20 and quits saving at the age of 30, leaving the money to grow. That's a total of ten years of diligent saving.

Person B begins saving $300 each month at the age of 30 and continues until the age of 65. That equates to 35 years of diligent saving.

Who will have more money at age 60 as a result of compound interest, assuming a 7 percent annual rate of return? Let's have a look:

	Initial Investment	Monthly Contribution	Starting Age	Ending Age	Portfolio size at age of 30 (at 7 percent annual return	Portfolio size at age of 65 (at 7 percent annual return)
Person A	$0	$300	20	30	$51,315	$547,868
Person B	$0	$300	30	65	$0	$513,424

Person A will end up with 7 percent more, or more than $34,000, in their portfolio than Person B while saving the same $300 per month. Person B saved $300 per month for 35 years, whereas Person A only saved $300 per month for 10 years. When you start investing early, compound interest can help you save a lot of money.

The majority of people are unaware of this financial prosperity secret. They believe that by saving more money later in life, they will be able to make up for it. However, by giving compound interest less time to work its magic, their total wealth will be lower.

7. You Will Develop Healthier Financial Habits

The start of your financial life can either be the riskiest or the most advantageous. This is the point at which you will begin to create financial habits. While the majority of people use this period to develop poor habits such as spending more than they earn or taking out loans to buy goods they can't afford, some will utilize it to develop good habits such as saving.

Debt is avoided by good investors because they want to earn interest rather than pay it. Because they enjoy having money to save and invest, a wise investor spends less than he or she earns. Successful investors cultivate patience because if they do not, compound interest will not have the time to build momentum.

BUDGETING

Making difficult decisions is an important part of growing up, and the sooner you make them, the better. While being a teenager can be a lot of fun, there are some duties that can make adolescence feel like a chore. It doesn't have to be that way, though. Money can become as easy to spend as it is to make despite not having a full-time job.

That way, when you start to assume more obligations like monthly bills and loans, you'll already have a firm foundation on how to budget your available funds. Here are some budgeting suggestions to help you make the most of your money.

1. Understand Your Income

Making money as a teenager is exciting, but you'll quickly realize that what you're promised and what you actually make are not the same thing.

When you get a paycheck, for example, you need to know how much money you will earn before and after taxes, which is known as distinguishing gross and net income. As a result, you'll know exactly how much money you're getting out of any salary you've made.

After that, add up any non-tax-deductible sources of income, such as gifts, tips, allowance, or bonuses. To be safe, total up the money you've received in the previous couple of months (just in case these statistics change over time). Divide that number by the number of months to get an approximation of your average monthly income, then work backward from there.

2. Project Your Expenses

The not-so-fun part now begins: creating a budget.

Layout any prospective expenses you may have for the month in question, just like you did with your income. Include payments for a car (gas, insurance, etc.), a phone, food and drink, grooming (haircuts, clothes, makeup, etc.), and any other living expenses.

Some of these costs will fluctuate over time. Having a monthly budget separate from the rest of the year will assist to alleviate stress.

Using an app is one of the simplest methods to keep track of your spending. Money Patrol allows you to automate the procedure by connecting it to your bank accounts. Create budgets for the categories that apply to your own spending, and you will have a better understanding of your spending habits over time.

3. Less is More (Spend Wisely)

You are entering a chapter of life where you'll make new friends, have eye-opening social encounters, and spend money on things you've always wanted. While spending your own money on the things you want is a good sensation, if it is mismanaged, it can have disastrous consequences for your financial future.

Credit cards can be both a blessing and a curse. A credit card is a convenient way to pay for anything when you don't have enough cash, and it also looks glamorous. But keep in mind that you still have to pay them off, which can be difficult if you aren't earning a good wage.

A prepaid debit card is a superior option because it teaches you how to manage your money without the hazards that come with a credit card. The Current Visa Debit Card is a wonderful option for teaching teens how to manage and budget their money while keeping parental controls in place. Furthermore, Current provides round-ups so that teens can increase their savings and set spending goals using an easy-to-use app.

4. If You Really Want It, Put Money Aside

Once you've survived puberty, you're basically an adult in training, according to Dave Ramsey, an American financial broadcaster and expert. You will learn how to become more self-reliant and spend your money on what you require throughout that training period.

Setting long-term financial objectives allows you to better manage your future expectations for those important life goals you yearned for as a child. You need vision to set your goals in motion, whether it's for your first automobile, a place of your own, or to start your own business.

5. Maintain Your Earnings

There is no such thing as 'too much work', no matter how old you are. Take on as many income-generating jobs as you can if you have the physical and mental capacities, so that saving becomes an activity that is natural for you.

Taking on odd jobs along the way can be beneficial. Taking on minor chores, such as mowing your neighbor's lawn, babysitting, tutoring, or simply shoveling snow from someone's driveway, will keep money flowing. If your neighbors or friends are too busy (or lazy) to undertake these menial jobs, they will seek assistance from you, and you will be able to earn some quick cash.

Any part-time work is also beneficial. The more active you are, the more likely you are to achieve the earning potential you desire.

6. Take Advice (Lots Of It)

It can be difficult to ask for advice. After all, adults are in no way perfect. They make many mistakes and if it was so easy, wouldn't they all be rich? This is all true, but it's for those exact reasons that they are an invaluable source of information on how to go about budgeting. They have experienced the highs and lows of financial management and can help you through them.

Your parents are a great place to start. They can help you make the most of any allowances or income you receive, so you don't have to rely on them for money at all times. Many will be very excited to help you prepare for your future.

Reading, on the other hand, is also quite beneficial since various sources will show you multiple opinions and ideas. Karen McGuire, a money columnist, published *The Teen Money Manual* to assist teenagers in learning more about money before they actually make it.

7. Learn About Inflation

Costs fluctuate over time, as previously stated. Due to inflation, what cost $100 a few months ago may cost $105 today. Inflation is a gradual increase in the price of goods or services that explains why you will have to pay greater prices in the future.

You can pro-rate future costs of items that gain with time using an inflation calculator like the one supplied by the US Bureau of Labor Statistics.

8. Divide and Rule

Still unsure how much money you should set aside for personal financial objectives and expenses? You don't need to be a math major, but percentages will come in handy.

A 50/20/30 split of your net income is one technique advocated at Money Under 30. The technique is as follows: you put 50 percent of your income toward fixed expenses, 20 percent toward savings and investments, and the remaining 30 percent into any sort of leisure you want to indulge in.

Sticking to a budget assists you to acquire financial discipline, so your parents won't be bothering you about how much you spend.

ADVANTAGES OF INVESTING IN YOUR 20S

Many young individuals appear to prefer deferring investment decisions until their financial situation becomes more stable, at least theoretically. Even with college debt and poor earnings, twenty-somethings are in a great position to enter the investment industry.

1. Time

Money may be scarce, but once again you have the benefit of time. There's a purpose Albert Einstein dubbed compounding, or being able to expand on an investment by reinvesting returns, the "eighth wonder of the world." Compounding allows investors to build wealth over time with only two requirements: the reinvestment of earnings and patience.

A $10,000 investment made at the age of 20 would have grown to almost $70,000 by the time the investor reached 60 (based on a 7 percent interest rate). The same $10,000 investment made at age 30 would produce around $43,000 at age 60, but just $26,000 at age 40. Money can develop more wealth if it is put to work for a longer period of time.

2. Take On More Risk

An investor's ability to tolerate risk is determined by their age, investment goals, income, and comfort level. People in their later years may prefer low-risk or risk-free assets like Treasury Bills and certificates of deposit (CDs) because risk-free assets are those whose future rates of return can be predicted with certainty.

This certainty is made possible by a high level of trust in the security's issuer. Young adults might develop more aggressive portfolios that are more volatile and have the potential to deliver higher rewards.

3. Learn By Doing

Young investors have the freedom and time to learn from their triumphs and errors while studying investment. They also have an edge since they have years to study the markets and develop their investing methods, as investing has a rather long learning curve. Younger investors can overcome investment blunders because they have the time to recover, just as they can tolerate more risk.

4. Tech Savvy

Due to growing up in the technology age, the younger generation is more technologically literate, capable of studying, researching, and implementing internet investing tools and approaches. Online trading platforms, chat rooms, financial, and educational websites give a plethora of chances for both fundamental and technical research. Other technologies, such as social media and various online applications, can also help a young investor expand his or her knowledge, experience, confidence, and expertise.

5. Human Capital

Human capital can be thought of as the current value of all future incomes from the standpoint of an individual. Young adults frequently have a plethora of possibilities to improve their capacity to earn greater future salaries and taking advantage of these opportunities might be regarded as one of many types of investment.

Because earning a living is a requirement for investing and saving for retirement, spending on oneself by getting a degree is a wise decision. On-the-job education or learning additional skills is also a wise investment that pays off handsomely.

WHAT IS COMPOUND INTEREST? HOW DOES IT WORK?

Compound interest (sometimes called compounding interest) is calculated on a deposit or loan utilizing both the starting principle and the cumulative interest over time. Compound interest grows at a quicker rate than simple interest, which is based only on the principal balance. It's a concept said to have started in Italy in the 17th century.

The compound interest rate is determined by the frequency of compounding; the higher the number of compounding periods, the higher the compound interest rate. Thus, during the same time period, compound interest on a $100 investment compounded at 10 percent annually will be less than compound interest on a $100 investment compounded at 5 percent semiannually. Because it can generate bigger positive returns based on the original principal amount, the interest-on-interest effect is known as the "miracle of compound interest".

THE MOST IMPORTANT TAKEAWAYS

- Compound interest is interest calculated on a deposit or loan's initial principal plus all accrued interest over a period of time.
- Multiply the annual interest rate by the number of compound periods minus one, then divide the initial principal by one.
- Interest can be compounded on a variety of schedules, including continuous, daily, and annual.
- The number of compounding periods makes a big difference when it comes to calculating compound interest.

CALCULATING COMPOUND INTEREST

Multiplying the original principal amount by one, then multiplying the interest compounded annually rate by the number of compound periods minus one, yields compound interest. The loan's total initial sum is then deducted from the final value.

COMPOUNDING PERIODS

Compound interest computations are heavily influenced by the number of compounding periods. The basic idea is that the more compounding periods there are, the higher the compounded interest rate.

The influence of the number of compounding periods on a $10,000 loan with a 10 percent annual interest rate over a 10-year period is shown in the table below.

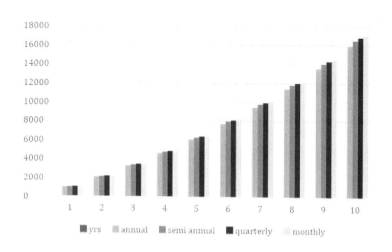

Compound interest can significantly improve long-term investment earnings. Over the course of ten years, a $100,000 account earning 5 percent simple annual interest would earn $50,000 in total interest, whereas a $10,000 deposit earning 5 percent compound annual interest would earn $62,889.46. The total interest would be $64,700.95 if the compounding period was paid monthly over the same 10-year period at 5 percent compound interest.

2

BEGINNING YOUR STOCK MARKET INVESTMENT JOURNEY

S tock investing can be a great strategy to establish financial security, but you might be asking how would you go about achieving it? This chapter will be going over the many ways to invest in the stock market and the things you should consider along the way.

HOW TO INVEST IN THE STOCK MARKET

You can get more active in stock investing in a number of ways. Choose the option that best describes how you need to invest and how hands-on you want to be when choosing equities to invest in from the options discussed in this chapter.

1. Make a Decision About How You Will Invest in Equities

I'm a "do it yourself" type that prefers to pick my own equities, mutual funds, and index funds. Continue reading to learn how to deconstruct the data that active investors need. If you already know how to buy stocks and only need a brokerage, the following list of the best online stock brokers is a good place to start:

1. Questrade
2. Qtrade Direct Investing
3. Interactive brokers
4. TD Direct Investors Edge

2. Open a Savings Investment Account

To put it another way, before you can invest in stocks, you must first open an investment account. This usually entails opening a brokerage account for the more hands-on sorts. Using a robo-advisor to open a record is a viable solution for individuals who only require a modest amount of assistance. Under the surface, the two operations are separated.

The following information is critical: you won't be able to buy individual equities in a 401(k) and your mutual fund options would be severely limited if you choose this option.

Just to mention, another way of saving is through RRSP. In Canada, RRSP is a retirement savings plan for both workers and self-employed individuals. Contributions can be made at any time and in any quantity up to a person's annual contribution limit.

While you have a restricted investment choice, a manager coordinating money makes it worthwhile to contribute. However, after you've provided enough to achieve that coordinate, it's no longer worthwhile.

Opening a robo-advisor account is a passive investment strategy. A robo-advisor provides the benefits of stock investing without the requirement for the owner to undertake the necessary research to choose specific assets like a mutual fund does.

Robotic advisor administrations also provide a comprehensive investment for the board of directors. During the onboarding process, these organizations will collect information about your financial goals and then put together a portfolio of investments to help you achieve them.

This may look expensive. On the other hand, the administrative expenditures incurred here are frequently a fraction of the costs involved with engaging a human investment supervisor. Most robo-advisors charge 0.25 percent to 0.50 percent of your profits under administration for this service. If you like, you can open an Individual Retirement Account (IRA) with a robo-advisor.

Another option is a TFSA (tax-free savings account). It is a type of savings account that is not taxed. Consider it to be a basket. You can choose from a variety of financial items to place in that basket, including stocks, guaranteed investment certificates, exchange-traded funds, bonds, and actual cash savings.

TFSAs were created by the Canadian government in 2009 as a strategy to encourage Canadians to save money and referred to as a "tax advantage account". You won't have to pay tax on the money you put into your TFSA because you paid tax on it when you put it in. TFSAs are tax-free accounts that encourage consumers to save for retirement or other significant purchases such as a home.

While TFSA donations may not provide immediate tax benefits as RRSP contributions do, you will benefit greatly in the future because all investment gains will be tax-free. To put it another way, because you have paid tax on the money you placed into your TFSA, you won't have to pay anything when you withdraw it.

TFSAs are excellent, but if you are not careful, they may get you into a lot of trouble. It is easy to lose track of how much you are contributing because TFSAs are so popular and plentiful, and you can open as many as you want. Even if it is by accident, if you contribute more money to your TFSA in a calendar year than you are allowed by law, you will be assessed a penalty of 1 percent per month on the amount in your TFSA that is in excess of the maximum.

Oh, and unless you want to face the wrath of the Canadian government's tax department, you cannot day-trade stocks in your TFSA.

3. Recognize the Difference Between Equities and Mutual Funds that Invest in Stocks

Will you be attending the DIY workshop? Make an effort not to be stressed. Stock investing does not have to be complicated or time-consuming. For the vast majority of people, investing in the stock market entails choosing between two sorts of investments called ETFs and individual shares of stock.

Mutual funds that track a list of financial organizations are known as record funds and exchange-traded funds (ETFs). These mutual funds allow you to acquire small amounts of a variety of equities in a single transaction.

A fund like the Standard & Poor's 500, for example, buys stock in the companies on the list. When you invest in a mutual fund, you become a part-owner of each of the companies included in it. You may put together a small number of funds to create a larger investment portfolio. It's worth noting that value mutual funds are another name for equity mutual funds.

For individual stocks of shares, you can buy a single offer or a modest number of shares to get your feet wet in the stock market before committing to a larger investment if you're interested in a specific company. It is possible to create a broad portfolio from a large number of individual companies, but it will require a lot of time and money.

Stock mutual funds are a good investment since they are diverse from the start, which lowers your risk of losing money. In any case, they are not expected to increase at the same rate that certain individual equities have in recent years.

Individual stocks have the advantage of being a solid investment that, if chosen wisely, may be highly profitable. On the other hand, the likelihood of getting wealthy through the purchase of a single stock is slim.

Building a portfolio mostly made of mutual funds is a sensible solution for the great majority of investors, particularly those investing their retirement assets.

4. Create a Financial Plan for Your Stock Investment

At this point in the procedure, a few questions commonly arise in the minds of new investors. For example, "What is the smallest amount of money I need to start investing in stocks?"

The price of a single share of stock determines the amount of money required to purchase it. An offer can range in price from a few dollars to two or three thousand dollars, depending on the terms. Meanwhile, an exchange-traded fund (ETF) may be the ideal alternative for you if you require mutual funds, but don't have a lot of money. Mutual funds typically demand a $1,000 minimum investment, whereas ETFs trade like stocks and can be purchased for a lower price (as low as $100 in some cases).

The next question you might ask would be "How much would be a good idea for me to put into stocks if I had a lot of money?"

If your portfolio has some long-term memories skyline, you may want to allocate a bigger amount of it to stock funds. A 30-year-old who is saving for retirement might invest 80 percent of his or her money in stock funds and 20 percent in bond funds or other investments. Singular stocks, on the other hand, are a very different animal.

5. Get Started With Your Investment

Despite the fact that there are numerous strategies and approaches to stock trading, the best investors have stayed faithful to the fundamentals and principles. That usually means sticking to money for the majority as part of your portfolio.

According to Warren Buffett, the best investment most Americans can make is a low-effort S&P 500 record fund. Individual stocks should only be chosen if you believe in the company's long-term growth potential.

If specific stocks present themselves to you, learning how to study them is a great investment of your time.

WHAT DOES A BROKER DO?

Your online broker serves as a link between you and the stock market. When you use an online broker to purchase and sell stock, your orders are routed to a market center where they are filled, and you receive the stock. Your brokerage account is where you keep all of your company shares until you are ready to sell them.

WHAT TO CONSIDER BEFORE SELECTING A BROKER

Before choosing a broker, investors should take into account a number of key factors.

Annual fees: In the United States, annual fees (sometimes known as inactivity costs or maintenance fees) are uncommon. However, in Canada, every broker charges them.

Questrade is the best in this regard, as an annual fee can be avoided by depositing $1,000 across all accounts. To avoid paying an annual charge, Scotia iTRADE, HSBC, BMO Investor Line, and CIBC Investor's Edge, for example, all demand at least $25,000 in RRSP accounts ($10,000 in non-registered accounts).

App availability on mobile devices: While every online brokerage in the United States has a mobile app, not every broker in Canada does, and the quality varies substantially in terms of functionality. Several of Canada's top banks, like HSBC and National Bank, do not provide clients with an easy-to-use and distinct mobile trading app.

Trading tools and platforms: Because they use well-known third-party suppliers like Trading Central and Morningstar, which are additionally extensively used in the United States, the biggest Canadian brokers do a decent job with stock research. However, the brokers' real trading tools and platforms can vary substantially.

Banking facilities: Banks that provide trading via the internet in the United States (for example, Bank of America's Merrill Edge) ensure a consistent client experience. Transferring funds between accounts, switching between bank and brokerage accounts with a single login, submitting tax returns, and other similar features are all required as a part of the overall experience in trading. In-person services at a neighboring branch office are also available. In Canada, the client experience varies greatly from one bank to the next.

Types of orders: Market orders, limit hours, and stop orders are all common practices in the financial business. However, what is available for trading US equities from Canada varies from broker to broker. This includes trading during off-hours. Conditional orders and other advanced order types will differ from broker to broker.

HOW TO SELECT A GOOD CANADIAN BROKERAGE

Beyond branding and marketing, Canadian brokerages strive to differentiate themselves from one another. What matters most, though, is the trading experience you have after you have a funded account. Here are some pointers to keep in mind while choosing a broker for the first time:

Know Your Account Type Beforehand

Do you want to open a taxable account or an RRSP (Registered Retirement Savings Plan)? If you're going to start with a standard account, as many investors do, at the very least look into the broker's RRSP options.

To avoid annual fees, verify the minimum account balance (or minimum trade activity) requirement, which varies by broker. This way, you will not be caught off guard when it comes time to register an RRSP account.

Does the Broker Offer Commission-Free ETFs?

Over the last decade, exchange-traded funds (ETFs) have become increasingly popular. There are thousands of ETFs to choose from, and many issuers (Blackrock iShares, Vanguard, and State Street Global Advisors' SPDR are the three largest) have partnered with brokerages to make their ETFs commission-free for customers.

They're available from Questrade, Qtrade, National Bank, and Scotia iTRADE. According to our analysis, Questrade has the finest overall selection of commission-free ETFs.

Check if the Asset Class You Want to Trade is Supported By Your Broker

If all you do is trade stocks, options, or mutual funds, then any broker will suffice. If you wish to trade sophisticated options, FX, or futures, you'll need to perform some preliminary study.

Read the Fine Print to Compare Potential Service Benefits for Active Traders

Being an active trader comes with a number of benefits, one of which is lower commissions. Some brokers will improve the quality of market data that is delivered to the account. Others will provide improved research tools or devoted client service. Because of its ultra-low trading expenses and outstanding trader tools, Interactive Brokers is the king among seasoned traders.

Customer Service

When calling a brokerage for account-related questions, all investors want quick response times and friendly customer service agents. Support quality and timeliness can vary, as they do in every firm.

Once you've narrowed your choices down to two, call both brokerages and ask them several questions. This little test could reveal a lot about what you can expect as a customer.

Tip: If possible, call as soon as the stock market opens. This is generally when support is busiest.

Account Security

Is two-factor authentication available? What is the security policy of the broker? How do you keep your valuables safe and secure on a regular basis?

STOCK MARKET TERMS FOR BEGINNERS

To begin, you'll need to grasp certain key concepts and phrases related to investing. Only the most significant keywords have been included, as there are so many that a book could be written about them all.

Share market: Investors and traders buy and sell financial securities in the stock exchange, which is known as the share market. By purchasing a share, you are making a financial investment in the company. As the firm grows, the value of your stock may rise as well.

Stock exchange: A stock exchange is a marketplace where companies' financial securities are purchased and sold. They are a part of the capital market ecosystem as a whole. After a company's securities, such as shares and bonds, have been issued in the primary market, they are traded on stock exchanges.

Over-the-counter: Over-the-counter trading is when you trade a security that isn't listed on a stock market.

Stock: A certificate proving ownership in a company is known as a stock certificate.

Share: A share of stock or a financial asset is a single unit of ownership. It is essentially an exchangeable component of a company's value that can rise or fall depending on a variety of market circumstances. As a technique of raising cash, companies divide their capital into shares.

Bull market: A bull market occurs when stock values in a market are generally rising.

Bear market: A bear market is the polar opposite of a bull market, and it occurs when stock prices in the market are generally declining.

Order: It's a declaration of intent to buy or sell stock in a specific price range. You can, for example, order up to 100 shares of Company A at $80 price per share.

Bid: The amount you are willing to pay for a share is known as your bid.

Ask: The price at which you are willing to sell a share is referred to as the "ask".

Bid-ask spread: This is the difference between what

individuals are prepared to pay to buy a share and what stockholders are willing to sell their shares for. This spread must be settled before a trade may take place. That is, if the lowest price for a share of Company A is $40 and the greatest price someone is ready to pay for such a share is $38, no trade may take place. Only when the bid and ask prices are equal can the deal take place.

Market order: A market order is an order to sell or buy shares at the current market price. Because the trade price might be quite variable, it is best to avoid making market orders.

Limit order: A limit order is an order to sell shares above a defined price or to buy shares below a set price. When trading stocks, you should always utilize limit orders.

Day order: A "day order" is an order that is valid only until the conclusion of the trading day. If the order is not completed by the end of the trading day, it will be canceled.

Liquidity: The ease with which a stock can be sold is referred to as liquidity. A highly liquid stock is one that can be sold fast and has a high trade volume.

Trading volume: Trading volumes refer to the number of shares traded on a given day.

IPO/Initial Public Offering: This is when a corporation first makes its stock available for trading on a stock exchange. Typically, you purchase shares from the prior owner of the stock rather than directly from the corporation. In the case of an initial public offering (IPO), you will be able to purchase shares directly from the company.

Market capitalization: The worth of a corporation on the stock market is known as market capitalization. That is the total current worth of all of its shares.

Mutual Funds: Mutual funds allow you to invest in a wide range of equities by pooling your money with that of other investors. Even if you just have a limited amount of money, you can diversify your investment this way. A fund manager is also in charge of picking the best stocks to invest in.

Exchange-Traded Funds: These are mutual funds that can be traded on the stock exchange like shares. Typically, they follow an index.

Index: A stock market index is a statistical metric that shows how the stock market is changing. In this approach, a stock index represents overall market senti-ment as well as the direction of product price move-ments in financial, commodities, and other markets.

Portfolio: A portfolio is essentially a collection of all of an investor's investments.

Intraday trading: Intraday trading is when you buy and sell stocks on the same day such that all of your positions are closed before the day's trading hours are up.

Dividends: A dividend is a portion of a corporation's profit that is delivered to its shareholders. When a firm makes a profit during a fiscal year, a portion of that profit is frequently distributed to its stockholders as dividends.

DIFFERENT TYPES OF STOCK YOU SHOULD KNOW

A stock is a financial instrument that allows you to invest in a publicly traded firm. When a firm sells stock to the general public, it usually does so as either ordinary stock or preferred stock.

The two most frequent stock kinds are common and preferred. Stocks are also divided into categories based on the size of the company, its industry, its geographic location, and its style. Here's everything you need to know about the various stock types.

Common Stock

If you are new to stock trading and want to acquire a couple of shares, you'll probably want to buy common stock. As the name implies, common stock is a type of stock that is traded on a regular basis and is the most common sort of stock.

You hold a share of the company's profits as well as the opportunity to vote if you own common stock. Dividends, which are payments provided to stockholders on a regular basis, are also available to common stockholders, but they are often variable and not guaranteed.

Preferred Stock

Preferred stock, the other major type of stock, is frequently likened to bonds. It usually delivers a fixed dividend to stockholders. Preferred stockholders are also given special consideration. Preferred shareholders get dividends before common shareholders, even in the event of bankruptcy or liquidation.

	Common Stock	Preferred stock
Pros	Long-term return potential is higher	Dividends are usually higher, assured, and fixed
	Right to vote	The price of a stock is less volatile
		In the event of bankruptcy, preferred shareholders are more likely to regain at least a portion of their investment
Cons	If dividends are paid, they are frequently lower, variable, and not guaranteed	Long-term growth potential is lower
	There's a chance that the stock price and dividend will be more volatile	In most circumstances, there are no voting privileges
	If the company goes bankrupt, the investment is more likely to be lost	

Preferred stock prices are less volatile than common stock prices, which implies preferred stock shares are less likely to lose value while simultaneously being less likely to gain value. Preferred stock is a good choice for investors that value income over long-term gain.

OTHER CATEGORIES OF STOCK

Different types of stocks are further differentiated in other ways within the broad categories of common and preferred. The following are a few of the most common:

Company size: You may have heard the terms large-cap or mid-cap before – they relate to a company's market capitalization or worth. There is a market for large-cap corporations valued at $10 billion or more. There is a market for mid-cap firms with a value of $2 billion to $10 billion. There is a market for small-cap firms with a value of $300 million to $2 billion.

Industry: Companies are often grouped into industries, which are referred to as sectors. In response to market or economic events, stocks in the same industry – for example, the technology or energy sectors – may move in lockstep. As a result, it's a smart idea to diversify your portfolio by buying companies from other industries. (Ask anyone who held a tech stock portfolio during the dot-com bubble.)

Location: Stocks are commonly categorized according to their geographical region. You can diversify your investment portfolio by investing not just in companies situated in the United States, but also in companies based abroad and in emerging countries, which are growing rapidly.

Style: Stocks are sometimes referred to as "growth" or "value" stocks. Companies that are growing swiftly or are positioned to develop quickly are considered growth stocks. Because they expect higher profits, investors are ready to pay a higher price for these equities.

DIFFERENT TYPES OF STOCK CLASSES

Companies can also categorize their shares into several classes, usually to differentiate rights to vote as a shareholder. If you possess Class A stock in a corporation, for example, you may have more voting rights per share than Class B investors.

Each class of a stock will normally have its own ticker symbol if the stock is divided into classes. For example, 21st Century Fox stock is traded as FOXA (A shares) and FOX (B shares).

CHOOSING THE RIGHT STOCKS FOR YOU

When it comes to stock investing, it's not so much about the stock's category as it is about whether you think in the company's long-term growth prospects and whether the stock fits in with your other investments.

However, if the prospect of putting together a diverse portfolio of individual stocks seems onerous – and it can be – you might want to explore stock index funds.

Index funds are one of the most straightforward ways to diversify your portfolio. These funds enable you to acquire a range of different stocks all at once. They follow a benchmark index, such as the S&P 500, to track a segment of the market, such as large-cap companies.

3

INVESTING IN THE STOCK MARKET

TYPES OF INVESTMENT VEHICLES

Stocks, mutual funds, bonds, and other investment vehicles are divided into a few basic asset groups. Asset classes are just broad categorizations or groupings of your numerous investing alternatives. Equities/stocks, bonds, real estate, and cash are the four major asset groups.

FOUR MAJOR ASSETS CLASSES

Equities/Stocks: This represents the value that would be returned to a company's shareholders if all of the assets were liquidated and all of the company's debt was paid off.

Bonds: A loan that you give to a business, government, or other entity.

Real Estate: A tangible asset.

Cash: Refers to having cash on hand or having money in a bank account.

Bonds and real estate are commonly referred to as "fixed income" (grouping them together). This is because they both create a consistent fixed income or payment over a set length of time (monthly, quarterly, etc.).

If you invest in bonds, you will receive a set income from the firm or government as it repays its loan with interest. If you invest in real estate, such fixed income could come from a renter or tenant who pays rent on a monthly basis.

When new investors have a long-term perspective before retirement, they usually invest heavily in equities. As an example, equities/stocks account for 90 percent of the portfolio while fixed income accounts for 10 percent (bonds and real estate).

FOUR PRIMARY TYPES OF INVESTMENT VEHICLES FOR INVESTORS

1. Mutual Funds

Mutual funds are investment vehicles that are managed by a professional investor with a defined investment goal. The sole function of that fund manager is to conduct stock research.

The fund's managers would then purchase a large number of various companies in order to diversify the fund's risks, and the fund would then be made public. Rather than buying individual stocks, investors buy shares in a mutual fund. The main benefit of investing in this way is that you are utilizing the fund management's financial experience.

Mutual funds have the drawback of employing a diversification strategy in their investments. You have put money into a stock portfolio, and some of the stocks are performing nicely. However, it is possible that one stock is gaining ground while another is losing ground.

In the end, your mutual fund makes a decent profit, but not as much as if you had individually invested directly in attractive stocks. Still, the benefit of mutual funds is that you do not have to worry as much. With the help of a manager, you can keep track of your stocks.

Another problem of mutual funds is that you must pay a management fee, which is frequently subtracted from the overall asset appreciation of the funds, as well as any expenditures allowed by law.

2. Individual Stocks

When a person buys a single stock, he or she is essentially buying ownership of that stock. If a person purchased 100 shares of a publicly traded corporation, he or she would own a proportion of the company. Companies originally go public to raise funds by selling shares to investors in order to launch, expand, and/or grow the business. Following the purchase of the initial shares, they can be purchased and sold on a stock exchange or between customers and vendors over the internet with stockbrokers assisting in the transaction.

Stocks can be used to create money in two different ways. One method is through stock price appreciation. Stock price appreciation occurs when the price of a particular stock increases. For example, if you buy a stock for $30 per share and it climbs to $39 per share after a year, the stock price has appreciated by 30 percent.

The other way to make money is through dividends, which are firm profits handed to shareholders.

The biggest benefit of investing in a single stock is that it has limitless growth potential. You can also purchase an income-producing stock. There may be some tax benefits as well. The stock appreciation is tax-free until it is sold, which is normally at a long-term capital gain tax rate if held for more than a year. Knowing your investment aim before buying a stock is crucial because there are several different types of firms to put money into, each with a distinct goal.

There are perils associated with any investment. Individual stocks have endless potential for gain, but they also have the potential for loss. If a corporation goes bankrupt, stockholders will almost certainly lose their whole investment. Even the largest corporations, as history has demonstrated, are vulnerable to bankruptcy.

Mutual funds, ETFs, managed accounts, and variable annuities are frequently used by investors who want to participate in the stock market, but want to limit some of their risks by diversifying their stock holdings.

3. Bonds

Bonds are a type of debt instrument. Bonds can be purchased individually or through ETFs and mutual funds. Bonds provide a lesser yield and are a safer investment than equities (you will get paid unless the underlying entity behind the bond defaults).

4. Index Funds/ETFs

ETFs and index funds are collections of assets that you can buy by combining your money with other investors. ETFs and index funds make diversification simple because when you buy a fund, you are buying all of the stocks or bonds in that fund. Without active management, these funds often reflect various markets and established indices.

The main distinction between index funds and exchange-traded funds is that index funds are traded like mutual funds, but only at the conclusion of the trading day, unlike stocks and bonds. ETFs, like stocks, move throughout the day. They are available for purchase and sale at any moment.

PERSONAL INVESTMENT ACCOUNT

It is a way to save money outside of a retirement account without having to use a cash account like certificates of deposit, savings, or checking. It can be opened in your name alone or jointly with others.

Where to Receive the Funds to Put Into the Account?

A personal investment account may be right for you if you have a windfall of wealth, an inheritance, profits from the sale of a property, mandatory minimum distributions, or excess income you will not need (for example, if you would not need the money in the next five years or longer).

Depending on the capital gains repercussions, you might potentially use existing holdings in a brokerage account.

Benefits

These types of investments have three tax advantages:

1. Rather than paying ordinary income tax on interest income, you pay capital gains tax on qualifying dividends.
2. On the earnings from your investments, you can pay as you go.
3. There will be a "step-up in basis" to your date of death for your heirs, which is the readjustment of the entire worth for tax reasons after you pass away. As a result,

the capital gains taxes owed to your beneficiaries are reduced.

COMMON INVESTMENT VEHICLES IN CANADA

Common investment vehicles in Canada include a registered retirement savings plan (RRSP) and a tax-free savings account (TFSA).

REGISTERED RETIREMENT SAVINGS PLAN

An RRSP is a government-approved account that allows Canadians to save for retirement. RRSPs, which were first introduced in 1957, are a tax-advantaged tool for individuals to save and invest their money.

Setting Up an RRSP Account

A financial institution such as a credit union, trust, bank, or insurance company can help you set up a registered retirement savings plan. Your financial institution may advise you on the various forms of RRSPs and the investments that can be included in them.

A spousal partner RRSP may be beneficial. This type of plan can help you divide your retirement income more evenly between you and your spouse. The benefit is greater if a higher-income spouse contributes to an RRSP for a lower-income spouse. The donor benefits from the tax deduction for the deductible in the near term, while the annuitant, who is likely to be in a lower tax band upon retirement, receives the income and declares it on their income tax and benefits return form in the long run.

If you like to develop and manage your own investment portfolio by purchasing and selling a number of various types of investments, you may choose to open a self-directed RRSP.

Taxing Of RRSP

Contributions to deductible RRSPs can help you save money on taxes. Regardless of how much money you make, RRSPs are usually tax-free as long as the funds remain in the plan. However, when you take payments from the plan, you will pay tax on the fund withdrawn.

When you contribute to an RRSP, your taxable income for the year is reduced, and you may receive a tax refund. You can put the money toward paying off a mortgage or other debt, saving for education, or other financial goals. In this way, an RRSP can assist you in planning for retirement and other objectives.

TAX SAVINGS ACCOUNT

In 2009, the TFSA program was established. It is a means for people who are 18 years old and older and have a valid social insurance number (SIN) to save money tax-free for the rest of their lives.

Contributions to a tax-free savings account (TFSA) are not tax-deductible. Even when withdrawn, any cash contributed as well as any income made in the account (for example, investment income and capital gains) are normally tax-free.

TFSA administrative or other costs, as well as any interest on money borrowed to contribute to a TFSA, are not tax-deductible.

Who Can Open a TFSA?

A TFSA can be opened by any Canadian resident who is 18 years of age or older and has a valid social insurance number. When you reach the age of 18, you will be eligible to contribute up to the entire TFSA dollar limit for the year.

The contribution maximum for a tax-free savings account in 2021 was $6,000, the same as in 2019 and 2020. If you have been eligible for a TFSA since its establishment in 2009, but have never made a contribution, your total contribution room in 2021 will be $75,500.

How to Open TFSA

At any given moment, you can have multiple TFSAs, but the total amount you contribute to them cannot exceed your allotted TFSA contribution room for that year.

You must accomplish both of the following to open a TFSA:

1. Make contact with your bank, credit union, or insurance provider (issuer).
2. Provide your SIN and date of birth to the issuer so that your eligible arrangement can be registered as a TFSA. Supporting papers may be requested by your issuer.

COMMON INVESTMENT VEHICLES IN THE UNITED STATES

Common investment vehicles in the United States include a 401(k), initial public offering (IPO), and an individual retirement account (IRA).

401(K)

A 401(k) is an employer-sponsored retirement plan. It allows a worker to set aside a percentage of their pre-tax income towards retirement. These funds are spread among a variety of assets, including equities, bonds, mutual funds, and cash. The term 401(k) is derived from the tax code part that established this form of plan, namely subsection 401(k).

How a 401(k) Works

Employers frequently provide 401(k) plans as a benefit to guarantee that employees have a source of retirement income. Each paycheck contains a percentage amount that is deducted and automatically invested in the employee's 401(k) account, as specified by the employee. 401(k) plans are made up of various investments that the employee chooses (typically stocks, bonds, and mutual funds).

It is possible that the money you invest will be tax-free and the employer may make matching contributions depending on the parameters of the plan. If your 401(k) plan includes either of those benefits, financial experts advise investing the highest amount possible each year, or as close to it as possible.

Benefits of 401(k)

401(k) tax advantages are hard to argue with because they may provide workers with a lot of financial stability, including:

a. Employer 401(k) Match

Do you enjoy getting free money? Now that we have gotten that out of the way, let's talk about what a company-matched 401(k) is. Many firms may match employee contributions up to a certain amount, either dollar for dollar or 50 cents for the dollar.

Assume you earn $100,000 per year and your employer matches 50 percent of your 401(k) contributions up to the first 6 percent you choose to contribute. If you donate 6 percent of your annual wages ($6,000), your employer will match 50 percent of that amount. So that is a total of $3,000 in your pocket.

b. 401(k) Tax Breaks

The tax advantages of 401(k)s are the equivalent of the gold medal in the financial world. To begin with, contributions are tax-deductible. The money is not taxed until it is withdrawn when you retire.

Second, because your 401(k) contributions are not considered income, you may be eligible for a reduced tax bracket. As a result of putting money aside for your retirement years, your tax burden will be lower.

Finally, your funds grow tax-free. Your net gains and dividends would be taxed in a traditional investment account. Your money grows tax-free in a 401(k) plan as long as it stays in the plan. This permits your earnings to compound.

c. 401(k) Shelter From Creditors

You will not have to worry about creditors going after your 401(k) if your finances take a turn for the worst. The Employee Retirement Income Security Act of 1974 (ERISA) protects your eligible retirement plan from judgment creditors.

IPO (INITIAL PUBLIC OFFERING)

An unlisted firm (one that is not listed on a stock market) wishes to raise money for the first time by selling securities or shares to the general public in an initial public offering (IPO). In other words, an initial public offering (IPO) is a primary market sale of securities to the general public.

The main market is where new securities are issued for the first time. After being listed on the stock exchange, the company becomes a publicly traded corporation and its shares can be freely exchanged on the open market.

The company that sells shares to the general public is known as the issuer. Initial public offers are divided into two categories:

a. Fixed Price Offering

A fixed price IPO refers to the price at which some companies offer their shares for the first time.

b. Book Building Offering

In the case of book building, the firm launching an IPO provides investors a 20 percent price band on the equities. Before the final price is set, interested investors place bids on the shares.

Small and medium-sized businesses, start-ups, and other new businesses use initial public offerings (IPOs) to expand and improve their existing operations. An IPO is a mechanism for firms to raise new funds, which can be used to fund research, fund capital expenditures, decrease debt, and explore other possibilities.

An IPO will also increase transparency in the company's operations because it will be forced to report financial statistics and other market-related happenings to stock exchanges on a timely basis.

After it is listed, the company's investments in various equity and bond instruments will be scrutinized more closely. Any company's IPO attracts a lot of attention and credibility. Client investment decisions are reported by analysts all across the world.

Advantage of Investing in an (IPO)

If you are smart and have some experience, you can make a lot of money betting on an IPO. Investors can make a decision based on the prospectus of the companies that are launching an IPO. They must study the IPO prospectus in order to gain a thorough understanding of the company's business plan and the reason for raising stock in the market.

However, in order to find opportunities, one must be vigilant and have a thorough understanding of financial conditions.

ACCOUNT FOR PERSONAL RETIREMENT (IRA)

An individual retirement account (IRA) is a financial institution account that allows a person to save for retirement with tax-free or tax-deferred growth. Each of the three primary types of IRAs has its own set of benefits:

- **Traditional Individual Retirement Accounts:**
  Individual retirement accounts allow people to make
  pre-tax contributions to a retirement account, which
  grows tax-deferred until withdrawal during
  retirement. Withdrawals from an IRA are taxed at the
  current income tax rate of the IRA owner.
- **Roth IRA:** This is where you make a contribution
  that has already been taxed (after-tax). As a result,
  your money can grow tax-free with tax-free
  withdrawals in retirement (if certain conditions are
  met).
- **Rollover IRA:** Money from a qualifying retirement
  plan is "rolled over" into this traditional IRA. Rollovers
  are the transfer of qualified assets from an employer-
  sponsored plan, such as a 401(k) or 403(b), to an
  individual retirement account (IRA).

Whether you choose a regular or Roth IRA, the tax advantages
allow your investments to compound faster than they would in
a taxed account.

DETERMINE YOUR STOCK MARKET STRATEGY

There are two methods to understand the dissimilarity between
short-term and long-term investments.

Any asset that you keep for less than a year is considered a
short-term investment. The great majority of investors only

hold short-term assets for a few months at a time, if not weeks at a time.

Any asset that you own for more than a year is considered a long-term investment. As part of their overall portfolio strategy, most investors retain long-term investments for several terms.

INVESTING FOR THE SHORT TERM VS. INVESTING FOR THE LONG TERM

How you use your investments determines whether they are short-term or long-term. In the hands of a trader, a stock is a short-term investment that will be sold in a matter of hours. Similar stock may possibly be regarded as a long-term investment if retained in a 401(k) for a number of years.

SHORT-TERM INVESTMENT

Short-term investments, as defined above, are financial instruments held for less than a year. The majority of traders will hold a short-term investment for a few months in the hopes of profiting from market instability and short-term gains.

While any asset has the potential to be a short-term investment, the vast majority will share a few features. They will usually be unstable assets, tolerating the price to fluctuate quickly enough for investors to earn from the asset in a short amount of time.

They will have minimal price fluctuations in most cases. Finally, a short-term investment will typically be very liquid, allowing investors to easily sell the asset.

Stocks, options, and exchange-traded funds (ETFs) are all volatile assets with established markets that allow for a quick sale. Day traders and active traders, in particular, frequently maintain considerable short-term stakes.

LONG-TERM INVESTMENT

Financial instruments that you retain for more than a year are known as long-term investments. Most traders keep these investments for several years, incorporating them into 401(k) plans, education funds, and long-term savings accounts.

Any asset, including short-term investments, can be a long-term investment. Long-term investments, on the other hand, continuously improve in value over time, making them ideal assets to own for a long time. Non-cash assets are frequently held by investors as long-term investments.

As Warren Buffett once said, "If you are not willing to own a stock for 10 years, don't even think about owning it for 10 minutes."

Real estate is the most prevalent long-term investment. Many people buy houses as investments to hold for years, if not decades, allowing the property's value to rise. The process of purchasing and selling a house, which is relatively non-cash, would make this a challenging short-term investment, but it would be less of a problem over time.

THE ROLE OF LONG TERM AND SHORT TERM INVESTMENT

In a portfolio, short-term and long-term investments play various roles. Among the more prevalent strategic distinctions are:

a. Volatility

Long-term investments tend to favor riskier assets, whereas short-term investments favor safer assets. While volatility isn't necessarily a good thing for long-term investments, it is usually a positive thing for short-term traders.

b. Small Movement

Short-term investments are more prone than long-term investments to seek out positions with fewer gains or losses. A trader has less time to regain any lost value from a short-term investment, therefore they prefer to invest in safer products that will generate returns in the near future. Those that hold short-term positions tend to make more frequent trades in order to compensate for lesser gains.

Day traders are one of the most common exceptions to this rule. They are more likely to seek high volatility swings, capitalizing on quick price changes in an asset over a short period of time.

c. Aggressive

Because long-term investments can bear losses better than short-term investments, they can be more aggressive. An investor who plans to keep a certain item for a long time has plenty of time to recuperate any lost value, which is typical with risky or aggressive acquisitions. This type of inaccuracy has a lot less place in short-term investing.

d. Passive Vs. Active Investing

Short-term investments are common among active investors. Because these traders' products are constantly changing, their assets are, by definition, short-term investments. On the other hand, passive investors are more likely to buy and hold assets for long periods of time. This implies that their assets are long-term investments by definition.

Active investing is a type of investment technique in which the investor buys and sells securities on a regular basis. Active investors buy investments and track their progress to take advantage of advantageous opportunities.

e. Immediate Vs. Horizon Goals

Investors typically select investments depending on their objectives.

Investors with short-term goals commonly embrace short-term investments. If they rely on the profits earned by their trading, professional traders, for example, usually keep short-term assets. In this case, the investor's aim will be to create money within a week or month.

Other investors may wish to increase the value of a vacation fund or save for a more luxurious vehicle. All of these holdings will most certainly expire within a year, thus they will mostly be made up of stocks, options, and other short-range investments.

Then there are those who seek to invest over a long period of time. These are investors that are putting money aside and trading for the future. Retirement funds and, increasingly, savings for a down payment on a home are examples of horizon goals. This position will not be closed out within a year by an investor. Instead, they plan to keep this portfolio for a long time. Long-term assets that expand over time are commonly used to fill that portfolio.

CHOOSING THE BEST STOCK TO INVEST IN

The following tools can be used to choose the best stock:

1. Price Earnings Ratio

P/E ratio is the abbreviation for price-earnings ratio. Many experts believe that this is the single most significant number to consider when buying a stock. While this is disputed, it is undeniably significant.

The P/E ratio is a single number that represents the outcome of some basic math. To calculate share earnings, you would divide the company's overall earnings by the number of outstanding shares. After that, the market price of the stock is divided by that number.

PE Ratio Calculation

$$\frac{\text{Earnings}}{\text{per Share}} = \frac{\text{Earnings (Previous 12 Months)}}{\text{Number of Shares Outstanding}}$$

$$\frac{\text{PE Ratio}}{\text{(Trailing)}} = \frac{\text{Share Price}}{\text{Earnings per Share}}$$

2. Earning Growth

Examine a company's net income increase over time. Keep an eye out for patterns. Is there a general upward trend in earnings? Even if the increase is not huge, a company with stable and unfailing income growth over time can be a worthy bet for the future.

3. Invest in a Company That You Are Familiar With

There are numerous compelling reasons to invest in well-known businesses whose products and services you are familiar with.

According to Warren Buffett, "Investors should stick to simple businesses that they understand." Warren Buffett is widely regarded as the greatest investor of all time, so it makes sense to follow his advice. It is easier to comprehend consumer-oriented firms that we use on a regular basis than it is to comprehend a large number of businesses that we never come across in our everyday lives.

In his renowned book, One Up on Wall Street, another extraordinarily successful investor, Peter Lynch, advises that ordinary investors may beat Wall Street by investing in companies that create some of the hottest new things they see in stores. If you have noticed that Costco products are flying off the shelves, consider finding out who makes them and investing in that company.

Consider how many people invested in Dell technologies, Raytheon technologies, JDS Uniphase, Yahoo, and a slew of other companies without understanding what they did or how they made money.

4. Volume

The evaluation of volume is one of these factors. The amount of stock purchased and sold in a single trading day is referred to as volume. It is critical to ensure that the total number of tasks exceeds 500,000. This is due to the fact that if the volume is low, liquidity is also low.

Because there are few buyers and sellers, low liquidity makes it difficult to buy or sell and causes the stock to move in a choppy manner. This causes a lot of unnecessary volatility, which is something a trader should try to avoid. This is the kind of bad situation that occurs while trading penny stocks.

INVESTMENT PORTFOLIO: WHAT IT IS AND HOW TO BUILD ONE

Investing, like any other industry, has its own lingo. The term "investment portfolio", which refers to all of your invested assets, is also commonly used. Portfolios of investments do not have to be complicated. To create a simple and effective portfolio, you can employ funds or even use a robo-advisor.

Although putting together an investment portfolio may appear daunting, there are actions you can take to make it easier. There is an option for you, no matter how involved you want to be with your financial portfolio. Consider your portfolio to be the foundation for achieving your ultimate aim of accumulating wealth.

Investment Portfolio Definition

Stocks, bonds, mutual funds, and exchange-traded funds are examples of assets that can be included in an investment portfolio. Although an investment portfolio is more of an idea than a real space, especially in the age of digital investing, it might be helpful to conceive of all your assets as being housed under one symbolic roof.

If you have a 401(k), an individual retirement account, and a taxable brokerage account, for example, you should consider all three accounts when deciding how to invest.

Investments Portfolio and Tolerance for Risk

When putting together a portfolio, one of the most important factors to consider is your personal risk tolerance. Your risk tolerance refers to how willing you are to endure investing losses in exchange for a larger probability of profit.

Your risk tolerance is influenced not only by the amount of time you have until you reach a financial objective like retirement, but also by how you deal with the emotional roller coaster that is the stock market. If your goal is several years away, you will have more time to ride out the market's highs and lows, allowing you to benefit from the market's overall upward trend.

Before you begin creating your investment portfolio, use a risk tolerance calculator to help you evaluate your risk tolerance.

TYPES OF PORTFOLIO INVESTMENT

1. Aggressive Portfolio

The phrase "no pain, no gain" is a good way to think about someone who wants an aggressive, growth-oriented strategy. This type of investor is willing to take on a lot of risk. They are unafraid of market volatility because they believe that what goes down will eventually go up, allowing them to profit from new opportunities during the upswing.

The phrase "eventually" is important to remember because a down market might take a long time to recover, which can be disastrous for someone who needs money right then. As a result, an aggressive portfolio necessitates a longer time horizon in order for the investor to have the time to adjust to any falls.

A risky portfolio is great for someone who is just getting started and wants to grow their money over time. They are more likely to produce higher gains if they start with a more aggressive approach, giving compounding time to work when your assets generate returns and (in many circumstances) dividends, resulting in a larger total that can subsequently earn even more returns. This phenomenon has the potential to significantly increase the value of your portfolio over time.

In an aggressive portfolio, newer or less-proven firms or industries are more likely to be included, as they have the potential for significant returns, but also large losses.

2. Conservative Portfolio

Someone who invests conservatively puts the preservation of their principal (i.e. their current funds) over maximum returns. This type of investor typically has a low-risk tolerance. In other words, they are willing to forego potentially large gains in exchange for more consistent returns, and they recognize that as a result, they will be less likely to encounter drops that would make them feel lightheaded.

When consumers have a short time horizon, they often choose a more conservative portfolio. The term "time horizon" alludes to how quickly you need the money, and a shorter time frame suggests that an investor intends to withdraw funds sooner rather than later. In that instance, stock market volatility could eat into their savings account, leaving them with insufficient time to recover.

While history shows that the stock market eventually rebounds and gains are returned to investors' portfolios, some with a shorter time horizon may be unable to wait. That is why a more conservative portfolio is necessary since it ensures that they will not incur large losses that will wipe out all of their savings.

A conservative portfolio is typically made up of safer investments like cash and bonds rather than stocks, which are regarded riskier because companies and industries come and go. When equities are included in a conservative portfolio, they tend to be large, well-known, and stable corporations (sometimes called "blue-chip stocks") that are less prone to undergo dramatic market volatility.

3. Moderate Portfolio

The goal of a moderate portfolio is to establish a balance between capital loss protection and significant investment growth. Moderate portfolios are more likely to have lower volatility than most broad equity market investment funds, and they frequently include a significant percentage of funds in asset classes like bonds that have historically predictable annual returns.

When compared to a conservative portfolio, moderate portfolios are designed to balance higher predicted growth with more volatility in potential returns year-to-year.

Bond ETFs will make up the majority of a user's portfolio if they have less than 5 years to attain their objective (90 percent or more). Stock ETFs will account for no more than 10 percent of the portfolio.

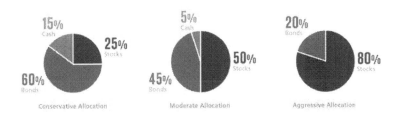

Conservative Allocation   Moderate Allocation   Aggressive Allocation

HOW TO BUILD AN INVESTMENT PORTFOLIO

1. Decide How Much Help You Need

You can still invest and manage your money if you do not want to establish an investment portfolio from the ground up. Robo-advisors are a more affordable solution. They build and manage an investment strategy for you depending on your risk tolerance and long-term objectives.

2. Choose an Account That Works Towards Your Goal

You will need an investment account to start building your portfolio. Investment accounts come in a variety of shapes and sizes. Some, such as IRAs, are designed for retirement and provide tax benefits for the money you put in. Regular taxable brokerage accounts are ideal for non-retirement objectives, such as a down payment on a property.

A high-yield savings account may be a better alternative if you need money for an investment within the next five years. Consider your investment goals before selecting an account.

WHY IS DIVERSIFICATION IMPORTANT?

Diversification is the practice of spreading your investments across different asset classes to limit your exposure to any one type of asset. This method is intended to help you lower your portfolio's volatility over time.

One of the keys to successful investing is learning to match your risk tolerance with your time horizon. If you invest your retirement assets too conservatively when you are young, you risk your investments not growing at the same rate as inflation.

Conversely, if you invest too aggressively as you get older, you risk leaving your savings vulnerable to market volatility, eroding the value of your assets at a time when you have fewer opportunities to recover your losses.

One strategy to balance risk and compensation in your financial portfolio is to mix your holdings. This strategy has a lot of different variations, but at its core is the simple idea of diversifying your portfolio across different asset classes.

Diversification in your portfolio can help to reduce risk and volatility, lowering the frequency and severity of panic. It is important to remember that diversification does not guarantee a profit or prevent you from losing money.

FOUR PRIMARY COMPONENTS OF A DIVERSIFIED PORTFOLIO

1. Domestic Stocks

Stocks are the most aggressive part of your portfolio, with the potential for larger long-term growth. However, this increased development potential comes with a higher risk, especially in the short term. Stocks are more volatile than other types of investments, so if and when you decide to sell one, your investment may be worth less than before.

2. Bonds

Most bonds pay a consistent rate of interest and are regarded as less volatile than equities. They can also operate as a hedge against the stock market's unpredictable ups and downs as they frequently react differently than stocks. Investors who prioritize safety over growth frequently prefer US Treasury or other high-quality bonds while minimizing their equity investment.

Many bonds, especially high-quality issues, do not give long-term returns as high as stocks. Therefore, these investors may have to accept lower long-term returns. However, some fixed income products, such as high-yield bonds and some international bonds, can provide significantly higher rates, though at a higher risk.

3. Short-Term Investment

Short-term investments include money market funds and short-term CDs. Money market funds are conservative investments that offer consistent returns and easy access to your capital, making them excellent for people who want to keep their money safe. In exchange for that level of safety, money market funds sometimes give lower returns than bond funds or individual bonds.

Because money market funds are neither insured nor guaranteed by the Federal Deposit Insurance Corporation (FDIC), they are thought to be safer and more conservative than CDs. When you invest in CDs, though, you may forego the liquidity that money market funds provide.

4. International Stock

Non-US company stocks frequently outperform their US equivalents, giving investors access to opportunities not available in US shares. If you are looking for assets with larger potential returns, but also more risk, try adding some international equities to your portfolio.

DIVIDEND INVESTING AND WHY IT IS A GREAT SOURCE OF PASSIVE INCOME

WHAT IS A DIVIDEND?

A dividend is a portion of a company's profits paid to shareholders on a quarterly basis, similar to a bonus to investors. Unlike stock prices, which fluctuate from day to day, a company's commitment to pay a dividend is virtually assured.

Dividends are a mechanism for shareholders to participate in and benefit from the underlying growth of the business in addition to the share prices rise. This wealth distribution might take two forms: cash dividends or equity dividends.

The majority of dividends paid in the United States are cash dividends, which are cash payments provided to investors on a per-share basis. If a corporation pays a 20 cent dividend per share, for example, an owner with 100 shares would receive $20 in cash. Stock dividends are an increase in the number of shares owned by a certain percentage. If an owner has 100 shares and the firm pays out a 10 percent stock dividend, the investor will finish up with 110 shares.

The payment of dividends is not assured. They are at the discretion of the board of directors. Unlike a bond, which must pay a set amount or face default, the board of directors can lower or even remove the dividend at any moment.

DIFFERENCE BETWEEN PREFERRED AND SPECIAL DIVIDENDS

While there are no guarantees when it comes to dividends, some are more important than others. Preferred stockholders have a greater claim on a company's assets than common stockholders, but a lesser claim than bondholders.

If a corporation is obliged to reduce its dividends, it begins at the bottom and works its way up. If there is any money left over, bondholders will be paid first, followed by preferred shareholders, and then common stockholders.

Companies use the same ladder to decide how to distribute capital in good times. Preferred shareholders are frequently paid first and receive a higher dividend than common shareholders.

The special dividend is another sort of payout. Special dividends are extra money added to your dividend cheque. They are a one-time dividend payment made by a corporation after a particularly successful quarter or when it wishes to modify its financial structure. Extra dividends are typically paid in cash and are generally larger than ordinary dividend payments.

WHY DO PEOPLE INVEST IN DIVIDEND STOCKS?

Despite the fact that dividends are not assured, they are relied upon by a large number of investors for income. Because corporations pay dividends at various periods throughout the year, retirees can set up a program to get a dividend payment every month of the year.

Younger investors, who may not require the income right away, might reinvest their dividends to put them to work right away in their portfolios. Dividend reinvestment programs automate this procedure, but your dividends are still taxed in the year you receive them, even if you reinvest them. Dividends in a tax-advantaged account, such as an individual retirement plan, are an exception because the money grows tax-free until it is withdrawn.

When interest rates are low, dividend stocks frequently offer larger yields than bonds, while also providing the possibility of the share price increasing. Even if the price goes down, a dividend can provide a steady source of income to a portfolio, and if you reinvest the dividends, a lower share price buys you more dividend shares.

WHY COMPANIES PAY DIVIDENDS

Dividends are often regarded as a sign of financial strength, therefore a firm may pay them to attract investors and raise the stock price. According to Matt Quinlan, who also oversees FRDPX, "A corporation that pledges to pay a dividend is frequently a higher-quality and more steady corporation."

Companies typically pay dividends when there is money left over after business reinvestment and operating expenses. As a result, established businesses are more likely to pay a dividend because they do not need to reinvest as much cash.

WHY COMPANIES DO NOT PAY DIVIDENDS

On the other hand, a young, rapidly growing company must frequently reinvest all of its resources to fuel growth and therefore cannot afford to pay a dividend.

Some investors like it because dividends are taxed at ordinary income rates. Investors benefit from a rising stock price if a non-dividend-paying company reinvests its money and grows, which is a profit that is not taxed until they sell.

To be able to reinvest or cover expenses, a mature company may decide not to pay a dividend. For investors, this could be a bad indicator, especially if the company is having financial troubles or expects future earnings to drop. When a corporation suspends or reduces its dividend, it is considered a bad indication, and investors will often sell their stocks.

As a result, you should be cautious when purchasing dividend stocks.

HOW TO SELECT THE BEST DIVIDEND STOCK TO BUY

The dividend yield, or the annual payout per share divided by the share price, is a frequent beginning point for these investments. The yield is a measure of how much money investors get back for every dollar they put into a stock. A 3 percent dividend yield, for example, would be a stock trading at $100 per share and paying a $3 dividend, giving you 3 cents in income for every dollar invested at the $100 share price.

The dividend is typically seen to be separate from the stock market's ups and downs, but the two are actually more intertwined than most people realize. When a company's stock price falls – as it typically does when it is in financial distress – the dividend yield rises. Investors who focus solely on the dividend yield risk missing the overall picture.

What investors truly desire is a combination of increased capital and increased income. Total return, or the growth in share price plus dividends paid, is what this is called. Investors should analyze what permits a company's business to expand so that its dividend may grow in order to select firms that are solid total return possibilities.

This may appear intimidating, but the procedure is similar to applying for a mortgage with a bank. Investors can analyze a company's financial accounts to see how it supports the dividend and if it can afford to continue paying it. This is just like how a lender looks at your bank statements and pay stubs to see how much money is coming in and if you can afford to pay your mortgage.

If a company's dividend is not funded through cash flow and operations, it is either going to deplete assets or borrow money to pay it off, which is not usually sustainable. As a result, the dividend will most likely be short-lived.

Dividends are given out of a company's free cash flow, which is determined by subtracting operational cash flow from capital expenditures. Companies that have a track record of generating free cash and returning it to shareholders over time will be in a better position to produce higher overall returns regardless of the environment. A healthy firm is the finest thing you can have in terms of having a solid, dividend-paying stock.

THE PAYOUT RATIO

To determine dividends that are sustainable, use the payout ratio. The dividend payout ratio, which measures the proportion of the firm's earnings distributed as dividends, is also available under company books.

The payout ratio is another measure of a company's dividend policy's long-term viability. A company that pays out too much of its earnings as a dividend cannot hope to keep its dividend and grow at the same time.

According to Brent View Investment Management's research, "Firms with the largest payouts and dividend yields not only underperformed the S&P 500 during the March 2020 sell-off, but also underperformed the overall market for the year. Furthermore, as the year continued, some of these same corporations slashed their payouts."

Dividend yields of 1 percent to 3 percent, along with payout ratios of 10 percent to 40 percent, should have a better chance of not only surviving in the short term without cuts, but perhaps thriving in the long run with dividend increases.

This low payout ratio benefits investors since the corporation may then reinvest the remainder of its earnings. If the reinvestment is effective and the business expands, the dividend paid the next year will be higher because the company's earnings for the year were higher.

LOOK FOR DIVIDEND GROWTH

A long-term dividend with room to expand is like winning the lottery. If you get both, you will be able to generate an ever-increasing income stream from the stock, something bonds cannot do because of their fixed coupon rates.

To locate firms with long-term dividend growth, look for companies that have more than doubled their payout in the last decade. This corresponds to a 7.2 percent annual dividend growth rate, which is significantly higher than the 3.8 percent annual inflation rate.

A dividend-paying stock that outperforms inflation can be compared to a pension with a cost-of-living adjustment. A payout ratio of less than 65 percent is likewise desirable.

Investors are not looking for companies that just increase their payout ratio to increase their dividends. It is all about the culture of continuous, consistent investments in profitable growth possibilities, which enables a steady stream of free cash flow over time.

The third filter is to keep a company's long-term debt-to-capital ratio below 50 percent or to exclusively use investment-grade debt. You do not want a corporation that overleverages itself and jeopardizes its dividend.

By limiting their investment universe to the highest-quality dividend payers, investors gain an advantaged starting position.

A corporation that can exhibit this track record has an ingrained character of resiliency. These are companies that have been able to sustain – and in some cases, enhance – their dividends during the course of the business cycle.

There will be times when a firm is unable to boost its dividend or can only do so at a reduced rate, but companies that pass these tests will be more stable and consistent dividend payers in the long run. The fact that FRDPX achieved a high single-digit dividend increase in 2020, while the S&P 500's dividend growth was basically zero, demonstrates this.

BE WARY OF CORPORATIONS WITH EXCESSIVE DEBT

Avoid corporations that are related to commodities or those that operate in industries with cyclical profitability and cash flow. In a negative cycle for that commodity or sector, they may not be able to continue paying a dividend.

You should also avoid corporations with excessive debt because this means that bondholders, whose interest payments must be made, have more influence over their financial withdrawals than stockholders whose payouts are elective. In a downturn, these companies may have to reduce their dividends to avoid defaulting on bond payments.

Of course, every company might suffer a setback, and diversity is the best hedging technique for an investor. Dividend income should be spread throughout enterprises and market sectors, according to experts.

DIVIDEND FUNDS CAN BE AN EASIER ALTERNATIVE

Investing in mutual funds and exchange-traded funds is a straightforward method to achieve a diversified dividend strategy. Active management is a feature of mutual funds, which means a professional manager actively selects the finest dividend stocks to invest in. It will also result in a greater expenditure ratio. Dividend ETFs are frequently less expensive because they do not have management hand-picking securities and instead just replicate an underlying index.

One downside to passive dividend ETFs is that their strategy may include rules that result in sector concentrations. If an ETF is overly focused on yield, for example, it is likely to be excessively weighted toward slow-growing sectors like utilities, consumer staples, or financials.

Dividend payers have had a revival in performance in 2021, especially when compared to non-paying corporations. The largest dividend ETFs have outperformed the S&P 500 to date, but it all hinges on their sector exposure. Financial ETFs, for example, have performed well when interest rates have risen, but other dividend-oriented sectors such as consumer staples, utilities, and healthcare have lagged.

An ETF, for example, may have a requirement that the companies it invests in have a lengthy history of paying dividends. This could cause the fund to overlook newer dividend firms like Apple (AAPL), which only started paying dividends in 2012. If the fund required ten years of dividend-paying history, it would still not hold Apple today.

HOW MUCH SHOULD YOU PUT INTO DIVIDEND STOCKS?

The percentage of your portfolio that should be allocated to a dividend strategy is determined by your risk tolerance, investing time frame, and income needs. Dividend stocks are not like bonds in that they do not promise that you will get your money back. Dividend investments, like any other stock, are vulnerable to market and company-specific risks.

Dividend equities are also subject to interest rate risk. Investors may abandon dividend stocks for the guaranteed income of bonds as interest rates increase, causing dividend stock prices to decrease.

BENEFITS AND DRAWBACKS OF DIVIDENDS

Dividend-paying corporations annually give a portion of their net income to stockholders and reinvest any residual earnings back into their operations. Thus, dividend stocks can be a fantastic way to add a bit of passive income to your investment portfolio because they pay out monthly cash dividends to their shareholders.

Dividend stocks provide a lot of advantages beyond passive income, but as with any investment, both the pros and cons of dividend investing should be considered before you make a decision.

BENEFITS OF DIVIDENDS

1. Generates Passive Income

Dividend stocks are popular among investors because they deliver a steady stream of income with little or no effort, similar to interest from a bank account, but with a higher potential for profit. You will make more money if you use your dividend gains to acquire more shares of a company's stock since each share you buy receives its own regular dividend distribution.

Although it may seem dangerous to expect dividend-paying corporations to keep up with their distributions, mature, well-established companies will go to great pains to not only keep their dividends stable and predictable, but also to grow the amounts paid out on a regular basis.

Dividend stability is one of the most significant variables in a company's ability to sustain a solid stock price, and dividend-paying corporations make it a point to do everything it takes to stay in good financial shape.

2. Utilize Compounding to its Best Potential

Compounding is a strong strategy to enhance your income by reinvesting your gains into new earnings. You can generate more money through compounding without having to invest any additional funds by just letting your earnings work for you.

This compounding technique takes advantage of the strength of increasing growth: your initial investment yields a specific profit, which can then be reinvested to yield even bigger profits. Thus, the longer you keep reinvesting, the faster your returns will grow.

3. Invest Once and Double Profit

When you invest in dividend stocks, you can benefit in a variety of ways. We already know that dividend investing has the potential to provide regular dividends, but there is also a return on investment when your stock prices rise.

Meanwhile, non-dividend-paying stocks can only be profitable if you buy them at a low price and sell them for a higher price. Dividend stocks, on the other hand, allow you to profit from the firm while keeping control of your investment. And, because a high proportion of dividend-paying companies are financially sound and dependable, their stock values tend to rise over time as their perceived investor value rises.

4. Dividend Reinvestment Might Help You Get the Most Out of Your Money

We all know that reinvesting your earnings is a great method to take advantage of compounding, but using a DRIP, or a dividend reinvestment plan, makes it much easier and more convenient.

DRIPs combine the benefits of compounding and dollar-cost averaging by allowing investors to reinvest their cash dividends into more firm shares on a regular basis. On a company's dividend distribution dates, these automated share purchases are usually made, and they can be administered either by the stock company or by an outside agent or brokerage.

Many DRIPs have the advantage of allowing you to buy additional firm shares commission-free or at a discount.

5. Tax Advantages on Dividends

Dividends are usually not taxed at the same rate as capital gains. First and foremost, you must assess if the dividend payments you are receiving are qualified or unqualified.

The income from qualifying dividends is taxed as capital gains. For most persons, the capital gains tax rate is either 15% or 20%, depending on their overall income. Because most corporate profits are treated as qualified dividends, you will be able to pay the capital gains tax rate, which is not only cheaper but also easier to manage.

There are certain holding requirements. To qualify for capital gains tax treatment, you must have held the stock for at least 60 days prior to the ex-dividend date. Unqualified dividends are paid by REITs (real estate investment trusts), MLPs (master limited partnerships), and BDCs (business development companies).

If you bought a stock less than 60 days before the ex-dividend date, the dividend payment will be considered unqualified for tax purposes, at least for that quarter. This means that any dividend income you earn under those circumstances will be subject to regular income taxes.

These tax considerations are unlikely to be significant for most dividend investors. Because you will have kept your investment for a long time before drawing income from it, all of your dividends will be eligible dividends.

DRAWBACKS OF DIVIDEND INVESTING

1. Twice the Taxation

One of the most significant disadvantages of dividend investing is that your dividend payments are effectively taxed twice. Because the firm that distributes dividends from its profit margin is required to pay tax on its yearly incomes, and it is these incomes that yield the company's dividend payments, before you receive your dividends, you will be taxed for the first time.

The second type of taxation happens when you, as a financier, must pay personal income tax on any dividends you receive throughout the tax year. In essence, double taxation means that you are taxed both as a partial owner of a business and as an individual.

2. Changes in Dividend Policy have Negative Consequences

The dividend policy of a firm is its plan for calculating dividend amounts and any prospective increases depending on future earnings. Thus, changes to a dividend-paying company's policy, particularly those that result in payout reductions or elimination, will have a negative impact on the stock price.

The clientele effect is a stock market idea that states that a stock's price is directly tied to the reactions of investors to business policy changes, and that when those changes occur, many investors would purchase or sell their firm shares in response.

If a company's dividends are forced to be decreased for any reason, you risk losing not only your regular share income but also your cumulative share appreciation when other investors sell and move on to other equities.

3. High Dividend Payout Risk

Investing in companies that have a high dividend payout ratio entails some risk. A company's dividend payout ratio shows how much of its income is distributed to shareholders against how much is maintained to pay the company's debt, reinvest in growth, and serve as a cash reserve.

Many firms find determining the amount to pay out to shareholders to be a tricky balancing act. They want to attract and retain investors with high payouts while also retaining enough revenues to enable future expansion and the opportunity to enhance dividend amounts.

Thus, when a company's dividend payout ratio gets too high to sustain, it may be forced to reduce or discontinue payout entirely.

BOTTOM LINE

Dividend stocks are less risky than non-dividend stocks in general. However, before attempting to include them in your financial portfolio, you should educate yourself on the pros and cons of dividend investing.

As Kevin O' Leary said, "I want to go to bed richer than when I woke up. The pursuit of wealth is a wonderful thing, but the thing is you have to be honest about it, you have to tell the truth."

5

STOCK MARKET STRATEGIES FOR YOUNG INVESTORS

UNDERSTANDING MARKET VOLATILITY AND HOW TO PROFIT FROM IT

Although stock market volatility may appear frightening, it is necessary for investors to succeed. It is why there are so many opportunities to buy fantastic stocks at low costs.

Before we begin, let's make sure you grasp the fundamentals of market volatility and the terms that are frequently used when discussing this topic.

DEFINITION OF MARKET VOLATILITY

How much does the stock market move up or down in relation to the standard? It is termed a turbulent market if it moves up and down more than usual.

When talking about market volatility, the stock market is usually what is being referred to, but it can also pertain to individual equities. The average movement of the market or stock over a set length of time determines what is considered "normal".

Market volatility is usually associated with danger, yet without it, investors would not be able to buy low and sell high as frequently. Before we get into how to profit from market volatility, let us go through the fundamentals of what market volatility is and how it affects stock market firms.

VOLATILE STOCK VS. VOLATILE MARKET

Volatility can refer to the market as a whole or to a single stock, according to the definition above. When we talk about volatility in relation to a specific stock, we indicate that the price of the stock is moving around more than usual.

Cryptocurrency equities, for example, are notoriously volatile with prices fluctuating substantially from one day to the next. If this pattern persists over time, it will be said to be less volatile because it is the stock's regular habit.

On the other hand, when talking about a volatile market, what is being referred to is substantial up or down fluctuations in the stock market as a whole.

We will utilize the S&P 500, which is a grouping of the 500 largest publicly listed stocks, to represent the market as a whole in this example. The stock market is considered to be volatile if the S&P 500 rises or decreases by more than 1 percent over a long period of time (which we witnessed during the COVID-19 epidemic).

Over the course of a day, both individual stocks and the S&P 500 bounce about. This is not considered a volatile situation. To assess if the market or a certain stock is acting volatile, pay attention to the prices at the close of each day over the course of a specified amount of time.

STOCK MARKET VOLATILITY INDEX

The VIX, or Volatility Index, was designed by the Chicago Board Options Exchange (CBOE) to monitor market volatility. Based on options traded on the S&P 500, the index reflects the stock market's 30-day projected volatility. When you trade options, you're basically wagering on whether the stock's price will climb or fall by a specific date.

The VIX is also known as the "Fear Index" since the higher the number, the more investors are betting the market will fall, increasing the risk. The S&P 500 generally decreases when the market volatility index, or calculated risk, rises. In the past, high VIX readings have signaled the start of a bear market (a prolonged period of decreasing prices).

IMPLIED VS. HISTORICAL MARKET VOLATILITY

The VIX is a measure of implied volatility. Implied volatility is a forward-looking indicator that uses buying and selling options to forecast future market or stock volatility. It calculates the market potential of an option and displays how much that asset could move – but not in which direction – up or down.

On the other side, historical market volatility assesses how volatile the market has been in the past. It is valuable for figuring out how much volatility an index or individual stock experiences on a regular basis, but it has no influence on how volatile it will be in the future.

It also illustrates the degree of risk associated with a certain item. If historical volatility for a stock lowers, for example, it indicates that there is now less uncertainty surrounding that stock.

WHAT CAUSES MARKET VOLATILITY?

Volatility in the stock market is mostly generated by uncertainty, which can be influenced by interest rates, tax changes, inflation rates, and other monetary policies, as well as industry changes and national and global events. In times of uncertainty, people are afraid of what the future contains, thus you can expect a volatile market.

At this moment, the government is taking a lot of monetary action, many industries and business sectors are changing, and there are all sorts of concerns because of the coronavirus. This clarifies what is causing the present market's stock market volatility.

HOW TO PREDICT VOLATILITY

While both implied and historical market volatility can be calculated, none can forecast future volatility. Market volatility would not have existed in the first place if the market was predictable.

In fact, because of this, volatile markets are even more unpredictable and risky. So the more important concerns are how to prepare for volatility and how you can profit from it when it occurs.

HOW TO PROFIT FROM MARKET VOLATILITY

While preparing for stock market volatility may appear like preparing for a storm you did not see coming, it is actually something investors should anticipate.

A turbulent market is an event that can present excellent investment chances. An event is something that occurs in the broader market that causes a business to be valued at a fraction of its true value. Because it imparts fear in the market, a turbulent stock market qualifies as an event, resulting in exceptional enterprises being valued at a fraction of their full worth.

When a company's price falls due to volatility, it is effectively "on sale" and investors can purchase it. When volatility appears to be going down, investors like it because they can purchase it, but they also enjoy it when it is going up.

BEST INVESTMENT IN A VOLATILE MARKET

When the stock market is volatile, the fact that a company's price has dropped is hardly an excuse to acquire it. Investing in turbulent markets can help you increase your portfolio quickly if you can locate companies with little to no debt, a demonstrated track record of success, and competent management.

1. Little to No Debt

When looking for the greatest investments to make in a turbulent market, one of the first things to evaluate is whether or not the firm has debt. In an ideal world, you would only invest in a company with no debt, but that generally is not a situation you will find yourself in.

Thus, you need to weigh a company's debt amongst its other factors. A lot of debt opens the door to probable bankruptcy in a volatile market, which is unpleasant. The more debt a company has, the riskier it is to invest in.

2. Proven Track Record

Second, the best predictor of a company's performance in a turbulent market is how it has performed in previous tumultuous markets.

If the market is extremely volatile, be aware that the company may have a difficult time and may suffer losses. Examine how the company behaved and recovered during previous periods of high volatility, such as the stock market crisis of 2007.

When the recession ended, did it prosper or struggle? If the company did well during and after the previous recession, it is a good clue that it will be able to do so again this time.

3. Strong Management

Finally, a great CEO (or a lousy one) can make or break a company's performance. It is crucial to trust the leadership with the direction the firm is taking any investment, but it is especially important when the market is volatile.

OTHER STOCK MARKET STRATEGIES FOR YOUNG INVESTORS

1. Value Investing Over a Long Period of Time

Although the value investing technique looks to be simple, it is more complex than it appears, especially when employed as a long-term investment plan.

As a result, practicing this technique is crucial. It is critical to resist the desire to make quick money by exploiting unanticipated market patterns, which can be very appealing. A value investing strategy is centered on buying stock in stable companies that will continue to be profitable and have their inherent value recognized by the markets.

Warren Buffett, who is widely considered as one of the twentieth century's best and most creative value investors, has said that when it comes to stock investment, "The market is currently a huge concern. A market can be used as a gauging machine in the long run."

Buffett chooses stocks based on a company's underlying potential and soundness rather than the market's cheap sticker price for individual shares of the company's stock. Rather than focusing on the cheap sticker price that the market has assigned to individual shares of the company's stock, Buffet evaluates the entire organization.

2. The Fundamentals of Growth Stock Investment Strategy

In terms of risk and reward, growth stock investing is essentially the same as value stock investing over the long run. A growth investing approach is one in which you invest in stocks based on an organization's intrinsic value as well as its ability to develop in the future.

Growth investors differ from cautious value investors in that they choose young enterprises that have demonstrated the ability to grow at a rate that is both necessary for the economy and better than expected. Firms that have exhibited signs of growth on multiple occasions, as well as considerable or quick increases in sales and profit over time, are attractive to growth investors.

According to the core premise underlying growth investment, an increase in share costs will be reflected in an increase in earnings or revenue created by a corporation. Thus, growth investors, as opposed to value investors, are more likely to buy stocks that are valued at or above an organization's current inborn worth because they believe that an organization's characteristic value will rise to a significantly higher level, well above the stock's current offer price, in the long run as a result of continued high growth.

The most prominent money-related measures utilized by growth investors are earnings per share (EPS), profit edge, and return on equity (ROE).

3. Get Familiar with the Stock Market

Stocks are little parts of a larger company. The stock price (also known as a "share") indicates the value of the company as well as the traders' opinions (traders and investors). Stocks do not have a fixed value; rather, they vary constantly throughout the day.

A stock exchange is where stocks are traded. Although some stock trading occurs outside of these hours, the majority of stock trading occurs during these hours. These hours are referred to as pre-market and twilight trading.

To research the stock and, finally, make a purchase or sale, you will need the "ticker" image. If the firm you are looking for is publicly traded, you may search for it in the results of your favorite internet search engine using the ticker symbol "quote" followed by the company's name, and you will almost definitely find the ticker image there. Tickers are a one to five-letter code used on the exchange to switch stocks.

For instance, the shares would be designated as Class A and Class B, and their company names would be displayed on the ticker with a lowercase letter to indicate that they were Class A and Class B, respectively. When a company's acronym is ABC, the ticker will read ABCa, and when the acronym is ABCb, the ticker will read as ABCb.

You can buy stocks with the intention of selling them for a bigger profit after a certain amount of time has passed, but this will come at a higher cost. In this circumstance, it is also possible to sell first.

Finally, there is the practice of short selling, which is popular among short-term traders but avoided by long-term investors. This is where an investor borrows a stock, sells the stock, and then buys the stock back to return it to the lender. Basically, they are betting that the stock they sell will drop in price and are trying to utilize that to their overall gain.

Before you start, learn about the bid-ask spread, which describes how money flows into and out of a market. Additionally, learn the ins and outs of viewing a stock chart and stock statements for information.

4. Successful Short-Term Investment Strategy

If you simply want to leave your money in the market for a short length of time before investing it elsewhere or selling it to utilize for other purposes, you will have to find alternative means to get the same level of safety and security that time provides in longer scenarios. Aggressive money-making tactics must be used to counteract this.

Income stocks, ETFs, and selected growth stocks are examples of a portfolio geared for short-term investing, but still constructed with a focus on safety.

5. Protect Yourself

Even the most experienced brokers with perfectly tuned senses are wrong from time to time. Companies with great potential do not always work out, and it is critical to have a plan in place to ensure that you are not out of the game for good and that your life remains manageable.

Do not put anything in the center that you cannot afford to lose, as the old poker adage advises. A well-planned personal budget is essential. You must first determine how much of your personal wealth you can invest. Do not worry if this figure is not as high as you would like.

Even if you can just invest a few hundred dollars per quarter, if it is well-managed and put to good use, you will have more money to invest next year than you had this year. Even if you start with a small amount, it is a lot better to start now.

6. Do Not Be Emotional

While this is not technically a plan, it is a crucial rule to remember. Investing based on short-term emotions is almost always a bad idea. Do not trade on the basis of a single article, one day, or a single drop. When an emotional buyer sees their favorite stock fall 10 percent, they may panic and sell.

A clever and diligent investor, on the other hand, will conduct research, determine that the 10 percent drop will have no impact on future performance, and then buy more shares. Those kinds of differences mount up over time.

If you cannot handle stock volatility and you know you are an emotional investor, you should change your overall investing strategy. Investing in stocks that are less volatile and have a higher resistance to market downturns might be a better alternative.

To limit the danger of a downturn in one section damaging a substantial percentage of your portfolio, diversify your portfolio and maintain some cash on hand. Just keep in mind that you should aim to avoid trading emotionally as much as possible.

7. Prices Do Not Matter

Another thing to keep in mind and put into practice is that prices do not matter. Stocks are frequently bought and sold based on their share price. You must recognize, however, that a $10 stock and a $1000 stock are not inherently better or worse than one another based on their prices.

If you put in the same amount of money, you will get the same result. Let us say 100 shares of a $10 stock and one share of a $1,000 stock are purchased. The $1000 stock may rise $100, whereas the $10 stock could raise $1.

Despite the price discrepancies, the 100 shares and the single share would both be worth $1100. This means that just the amount of money invested matters, not the price. In truth, a stock's price is meaningless in and of itself because prices are frequently adjusted owing to stock splits.

If you cannot buy a costly stock, that's great; nevertheless, keep in mind that the price of a stock does not mean anything. Fun fact: BRK.A, one of Berkshire Hathaway's equities, is now trading in the hundreds of thousands of dollars.

8. What To Do When Everything Seems To Be Falling Apart

Regrettably, not everything rises all of the time. If there is a market correction or crash, the entire market may fall. Knowing what to do in these situations can save you money as well as make you money.

To start, keep in mind that bear markets and corrections have historically been short-lived. Basically, you could ignore a crash during most bear markets throughout history and your portfolio would recover within five years.

As a result, the best way to profit from falling stock prices is to keep your key investments, raise some cash, and buy the greatest deals as near to the markets as possible. To put it another way, sell stocks that will recover the slowest or have dropped the farthest and then purchase stocks around their lows that have gone the longest and are expected to recover the fastest.

For example, during the 2020 fall, I purchased significantly into Tesla (TSLA) around its $350 low and up to $550 because I am confident that Tesla's stock will be back to its near $1000 high within five years. On the other hand, I will sell a recession-proof stock like Johnson & Johnson (J&J), which won't change much.

This way, I can take advantage of a market drop and maybe profit. This strategy assumes that the market will recover swiftly, whereas an economic downturn would be a different story. Also, if you have enough cash to take advantage of any opportunities, it is acceptable to hold stocks that do not move much, such as J&J.

To determine which stocks will regain the most, you must first determine which stocks have lost the most value simply because the market has declined rather than because of a genuine company issue that contributed to the crash or correction.

Tesla, for example, lost more than 60 percent of its value between 2009 and 2020, falling from roughly $950 to $350. At the same time, Carnival (CCL), a cruise tour operator, saw its stock fall from a high of almost $50 to just under $10, resulting in an 80 percent drop in share value. While Carnival may appear to be a better deal than Tesla, Carnival is considerably more harmed by the crash's core cause than Tesla. As a result, it may be more advantageous to invest in Tesla because the company is more likely to recover faster.

So, when is the best time to buy? The most important thing to know is that it is totally fine not to time the bottom of a crash properly. It is preferable to purchase a Tesla for $500 and ride it to $900 than to try and fail to buy it for $300 and lose out on the profit. Buying at a discount of 5 percent to 10 percent off a market's bottom will still yield higher gains in a few years than not buying at all.

It is rather simple to identify when the worst of a fall has passed, such as after a 30 percent loss in a week. Even if the market drops another 10 percent following its 30 percent drop, buying would still be within the suggested buy-in range of 5 percent to 10 percent off the low during a crash or correction.

To summarize, stay calm and avoid being emotional. The advice above has historically allowed for the highest profits during a crash or correction, but each case is unique, so you may need to make your own selections based on your own circumstances. Finally, keep in mind that neither a bull market (in which the price of a stock is expected to rise) nor a down market can persist indefinitely.

9. The Rule of Opposites

Starting with the law of opposites, it is vital to understand some fundamental rules, concepts, and techniques that influence when to purchase and sell stocks. The law of opposites states that a wise investor will do the opposite of the market in most cases. This only applies to money invested in short-term holdings, such as equities purchased with the intention of selling within a year.

The law of opposites states that if the market is rising, an investor should sell gradually. And in turn, that an investor should gradually buy if the market is falling. Markets that are rising will almost certainly face a correction (a short-term slump) during the next five years. This is based on the simple premise that if everyone is making money, it cannot last.

The crash of the housing market and, with it, the stock market, demonstrated this in 2008. The economy cannot continue to earn money for all parties involved indefinitely, necessitating corrections and collapses.

However, in the past, US stock markets have seen extraordinarily extended bull markets, the most recent of which lasted eleven years. As a result, a wise investor will not sell all, or even most, of his or her holdings during a bull market.

It is also not advisable to sell money invested in dividend stocks or companies purchased for the long term. Stocks are rising simply because the market is rising, and risky investments are excellent investments to sell gradually as the market rises. For every 10 percent increase in the stock market, you might sell 5 percent of your shares and keep the rest in cash. You might also attempt day trading with part of the money you would ordinarily keep in cash.

As previously said, the market does not always rise. Corrections are almost certain to occur. Dips in the market, on the other hand, should not be viewed negatively. Instead, they should be considered as purchasing opportunities. The US market has had 32 bear markets in the last decade. They happen every 3 to 4 years on average and last just over a year.

Remember that a year is little to a long-term investor. Most markets soon recover from declines and surge to even higher levels. As a result, a wise investor will buy as the market falls.

For example, if the market falls by 5 percent, you should invest 10 percent of your wealth (or 10 percent of your cash). Because market corrections typically erase 13 percent of a market's value, a one-year recession followed by a two-year comeback might result in 20 percent of a portfolio gaining 20 percent more profit.

10. Understanding the Economy

It is critical to know which stocks are good and which are poor to buy at any given time in the economy. Stocks that offer necessities like toilet paper, clothes, medical supplies (such as Band-Aids), and food are the best investments during economic downturns.

During a correction, these types of stocks frequently rise. Johnson & Johnson (JNJ), a medical device and pharmaceuticals company, Ross Stores (ROST), a bargain clothing retailer, and Walmart (WMT), a discount store chain, are all examples.

Invest some money in stocks with great growth potential during a booming economy. A strong economy can operate as a safety blanket, propelling stocks that would otherwise under-perform.

So, have a look at the economy in your area. Do some research to determine which stocks are best positioned to profit from your country's current scenario. If you have done your homework and established that an international company is a good investment, possibly because of its country's economic circumstances, you might want to consider investing in foreign stocks.

To summarize, be aware of your surroundings and take appropriate action.

11. Invest In Damaged Stocks Rather Than Damaged Companies

The difference between a damaged stock and a damaged company is the difference between making and losing money, and knowing the difference is crucial. Companies that have been damaged or have had long-term income, reputation, or product losses can take years to recover from. Meanwhile, stocks that have been damaged have fallen as a result of a short-term occurrence or even something wholly unrelated to the company.

Chipotle, for example, once unintentionally spread a virus through its meal. Its stock took huge damage as a result of this, as well as its reputation and sales. Chipotle would have been a damaged firm and a bad investment at that time.

However, consider the case of a celebrity who ordered Chipotle and developed an adverse reaction. The company was then attacked on social media by that celebrity, resulting in a 10 percent drop in the stock price. Chipotle would be considered a damaged stock and hence a good prospective purchase in this case because the allergic reaction does not indicate any concerns with the firm.

Use this rule of thumb to decide whether a company's problems make it a good investment.

13. Cutting Losses

Having rules on when to sell a stock if it is losing money is a proven way to avoid losing money. For example, I have a ten percent guideline in place. Every time I buy a stock, I will place an infinite sell order for 10 percent less than the price I paid. If the stock falls 10 percent, I will cut my losses.

Unfortunately, this strategy can backfire on occasion. Stocks could drop 10 percent before rebounding to fresh highs. However, I believe that the 10 percent rule saves more losses than it preserves gains. Set a sell order 20 percent below, or 30 percent below, the current price if you trust in a company, but know it is volatile. This type of rule is merely a smart precaution to have in place.

14. Trade What You Know

Trading what you know and what is around you is a wonderful rule of thumb for making effective investments. This may be the newest fad at school for an adolescent. Identifying trends before they reach their peak and investing in firms that will benefit from the trend can lead to some excellent investments.

Always be on the lookout for new items and ideas, whether at work, at home, in a mall, or online. Identify potential investments using your individual skills and knowledge. If you enjoy gaming and have heard that a new game is about to revolutionize the industry, look up the firm that made it. Trading what you know and identifying trends before they take off can result in significant profits.

15. Diversify

As previously mentioned, individual segments, industries, or equities might experience downturns even if the market as a whole does not. As a result, diversifying your portfolio is critical to reducing the chance of a catastrophic loss due to a single incident. For example, as electric cars grow more common, a portfolio invested solely in gas station companies could suffer significant losses.

Make sure to research industry cycles and diversify based on that knowledge. Invest in a variety of industries, firms of all sizes, and organizations with varying levels of risk. Diversifying your portfolio reduces overall risk and creates a more stable portfolio.

IMPORTANCE OF TIME IN THE MARKET VS. TIMING THE MARKET

You may have heard a buddy brag about purchasing a stock prior to it tripling in value, however, as Warren Buffett famously stated, "The basic purpose of stock projections is to make fortune-tellers appear good." Smart investors understand that predicting the performance of a stock is impossible.

Any stock can result in a profit or loss, but the desire to "strike it big" in the markets has prompted many investors to attempt market timing. When it comes to investing, there is always a dispute about whether it is better to stay in the market or to time the market.

WHY TIME IN THE MARKET BEATS MARKET TIMING

A stock buyer tries to forecast the future market price of a stock when attempting to time the market. Meanwhile, if an investor wants to build wealth over time, they buy equities rather than attempting to predict when the market will be at its lowest and highest points.

That begs the question: which one produces better results?

WHAT IS TIMING THE MARKET?

Timing the market entails attempting to forecast the future. This method, however, has a high chance of failing because no one has a crystal ball. Buying stock and then selling it for a profit seems ideal, but it is often too good to be true. People get lucky all the time, but that is precisely what it is: just luck.

Another fact is that consistently timing the market is very difficult. This means that someone may strike it rich with one stock, but lose everything on the next.

There are also other unanticipated financial consequences with timing the market. Frequent trading increases brokerage commission charges when working with a broker. Your broker makes more money the more stocks you buy and sell. Also, regardless of whether the investment makes a profit or not, the commission must be paid.

DOES TIMING THE MARKET WORK?

It is virtually impossible to establish whether security has reached its lowest or highest position with any degree of accuracy or consistency. Predicting the future is financially dangerous, and anyone who suggests it should be wary of any financial advisor who does it, as it displays poor judgment and mismatched interests. You have to do your homework and research stocks in order to select the best ones for your portfolio.

TIME IN THE MARKET IS THE KEY TO LONG-TERM WEALTH

Time in the market, as opposed to market timing, does not rely on short-term forecasts. This technique demonstrates that in the market, time and patience are preferable to a rapid sale. When you own a stock for ten years, for example, the beneficial effects of compounding and investment growth reap enormous benefits. By allowing your investments to expand over time, patient investors profit more.

Spending time in the market is the key to building long-term wealth. As a result, you are able to ride out the normal market cycles. Some people find it difficult to devote that much time to the stock market, but they should keep in mind how it relates to their financial objectives. Perhaps they are aware that they will require the funds for retirement or even the purchase of a home.

Smart investors can attain their long-term financial goals by waiting for steady growth over time, as indicated in their financial plan.

6

COMMON INVESTING MISTAKES TO AVOID AS A BEGINNER

Iff you have been saving for a time, you are likely to have a significant sum of money to invest. The goal of investing your funds is to generate a consistent income stream that keeps up with inflation. However, this also entails confronting the challenges of investment losses, stock market crashes, and economic downturns.

Do not be concerned! This book explains the most typical mistakes made by first-time investors and offers advice on how to avoid losing your hard-earned money during difficult economic times.

WHAT ARE EMOTIONS?

Any brief conscious experience is marked by intense mental activity and a strong sense of pleasure or unhappiness. Mood, temperament, personality, disposition, and motivation are all connected with emotion.

Cognition, according to certain ideas, is an important part of emotion. Those who act largely on their emotions may appear to be doing without thinking, but mental processes are still necessary, especially in the interpretation of events.

The understanding that we are in a dangerous position, as well as the following stimulation of our nervous system (rapid heartbeat and breathing, sweating, muscle tightness, etc.) are all part of the experience of being terrified. On the other hand, other theories claim that emotion exists independently of intellect and can even come before it.

THE IMPACT OF EMOTION WHEN INVESTING

Emotions have two distinct effects on the investment process. As an investor, you make emotional decisions that can have a significant impact on investing results. For example, you prefer to focus on short-term volatility and invest in low-return stocks to alleviate this emotional aspect. You stick to equities (stocks) that you are familiar with, but take no risks. Long-term investment can suffer as a result. It's good to have a guided balance between emotional purchasing and emotional selling.

Second, prices rarely reflect underlying fundamentals since the stock market is dominated by emotional crowds. Your goal is to develop a value investing approach that allows you to profit from the consequent price distortions caused by emotional factors.

To expand on this concept, you are not attempting to outwit or out-analyze other investors; rather, you are attempting to find behavioral pricing distortions that might be exploited. As a result, you are frequently taking positions that are distinct from, and sometimes even contradictory to, the emotive masses that caused the pricing distortions in the first place.

As a result, good value investing necessitates the management of emotions in two ways:

1. You must maintain emotional control throughout the investment process.
2. You must use an approach that objectively identifies price distortions that can be exploited to generate higher results.

BASIC CONCEPT IN EMOTIONAL CONTROL

The purpose of stock investment is to accumulate as much wealth as possible, and becoming affluent is perfectly acceptable. I am surprised I have to say this, but I have encountered a lot of people who find it difficult to admit they want to be wealthy and build their fortune. Give yourself permission to be wealthy because this emotion can have a significant detrimental impact on long-term wealth.

When making investment decisions, avoid using statements like "I think", "I feel", or "my intuition tells me". Create a procedure that is objective and involves as little subjectivity as feasible. Make decisions based on a thorough and comprehensive analysis. This is the most effective method of removing feelings.

This does not mean that emotions must be completely eradicated, as they are an integral part of human nature and hence play a crucial role in our daily decision-making. When it comes to stock selecting, though, mastering your emotions is crucial. These suggestions are made because I feel they are the most reliable path to improved returns. Individuals make decisions based on emotions and anecdotal knowledge, according to a significant corpus of behavioral studies.

While you may utilize an emotive, anecdotal approach when making day-to-day decisions, you will underperform when it comes to investing. When it comes to stock selection, you are not putting together a group of friends or relatives, but rather determining the best possible stock combination for creating the highest potential return.

Do not fall in love with your stocks and then be disappointed when they fail to satisfy your expectations.

Sell them without remorse if they do not meet your standards. Stay in the moment when making investment decisions. Do not obsess over past choices. Based on the knowledge available at the time, make the best judgment you can. Some choices will outperform others in terms of returns. Accept the truth that it is impossible to predict whether a stock will be a winner or a loser at the moment the investing choice is made. You can only hope to change the odds in your favor.

As a result, unsuccessful investment decisions are not mistakes, but rather an expected part of the investing process. Spend no time or energy wallowing in sorrow or second-guessing past actions. Stay in the present moment at all times.

When it comes to stocks, there are a lot of risks, but a closer look reveals that what many people consider risk is actually an emotional reaction to fluctuation. According to behavioral science, we are predisposed to feel twice as horrible about a loss as we do about a gain of equal value.

We also have a hard time focusing on the long term and prefer to judge performance over short periods of time. This causes skewed risk perception and, as a result, a decrease in long-term wealth. Volatility, as it turns out, has relatively little impact on long-term wealth. As a result of removing emotions from the investment process, emotionally charged volatility is often ignored. Volatility and risk are not the same, so do not use the terms interchangeably when discussing stock risk.

Instead, you should concentrate on the commercial and economic drivers of risk. Short-term volatility should be mostly ignored in such conversations since it plays almost no effect in stock selection decisions due to the fact emotions are ruthlessly removed from the investment process. Some of you may believe that investing should be about more than merely maximizing profits.

To summarize, get affluent first, then do good. Do not let your good intentions influence your investment decisions. When you apply these principles to your investment decisions, you will be on your way to mastering your emotions.

INVESTING IN A BUSINESS YOU DO NOT UNDERSTAND

One of the most typical mistakes made by first-time investors is to invest in a company whose business model they are unfamiliar with. This can be a costly mistake because you need to know how a firm works in order to assess its possibilities. Many beginner investors are more interested in the hoopla surrounding a company's business plan than in understanding its business model, which might cost them in the long run.

Before investing in a firm, an astute financial investor will evaluate its financial performance and revenue. They will make their ultimate judgment based on facts and figures, rather than hearsay and gossip in the marketplace. This advice comes from Warren Buffet, a billionaire and one of the world's most successful investors.

If you do not want to go into the details of each company, but still want a well-diversified portfolio, mutual funds or exchange-traded funds are the way to go. However, if you are interested in buying individual stocks from a potential company, make sure you do your homework and know what the company is all about.

FAILURE TO DIVERSIFY

To reduce your risks as a beginning investor, you should diversify your portfolio. You can do this by putting together a well-balanced mutual fund or exchange-traded fund portfolio. Questrade, one of Canada's leading online brokerages, is recommended for people wishing to invest on their own and conduct some DIY (Do It Yourself) investing. Not only is their platform simple to use and navigate, but they also offer a variety of research alternatives to help you build your own portfolio.

If you are not comfortable with the thought of doing your own investing, a robo-advisor can help you start with a balanced and diversified portfolio based on your risk tolerance. Wealthsimple is now at the top of the list with its great layout and wide range of features.

Seasoned investors can make informed selections about particular stocks based on their knowledge and experience. New investors try to imitate this, but often end up losing a lot of money. Individual stocks should never be purchased if you are new to trading. Only the most experienced investors should engage in such high-risk trading since they possess the necessary information and abilities. For rookie investors, the saying "do not put all your eggs in one basket" appears to be especially true.

You can then attempt investing in particular equities as you develop experience and information about the basics of investment. Initially, this should only account for a small portion of your overall portfolio. Even so, you should aim to diversify your portfolio by investing in all key areas. As a general rule, do not put more than 5 percent of your money into any single asset.

If some sectors do poorly, this investment technique has the ability to reduce losses. When certain industries experience a slowdown, other sectors frequently outperform them. As a result, even if the economy is sluggish, diversification can lead to fewer overall losses across all businesses.

Diversification, in the same way that it reduces risk, can also result in a lower yield. This is undeniably true as decreased risk equates to lower profits. However, given that equities have traditionally gained at a 10 percent annual pace, the overall rate of return on your investment will be fairly good.

This average takes into consideration all the big financial crises and recessions. A 10 percent rate of return is fairly decent in terms of portfolio performance. For first-time investors, this is a great place to start. You need to learn the know-how and abilities required for high-risk trading in order to achieve significant returns.

HIGH INVESTMENT TURNOVER

The rate at which a security holder sells securities is referred to as investment turnover. For instance, if a mutual fund holds $100 million in equities and sells $30 million worth of assets over a given year, the investment turnover is 30 percent.

High investment turnover is not a good idea because it results in higher transaction costs, which can outweigh investment profits. High-turnover investment funds are not a suitable choice for investors. Actively managed portfolios, on the other hand, have a higher turnover rate than passive funds.

Unless you're an institutional investor with access to cheap commission rates, high investment turnover is not recommended. The transaction expenses and taxes will be excessive in this instance. There is also the possibility of lost earnings (opportunity cost) as you will miss out on rewards if the stock you sold appreciates steadily over time.

Jumping from one financial product to the next does not provide strong long-term results.

MARKET TIMING

This prevalent misunderstanding is linked to investment turnover. Although some active traders promote market timing, one thing is certain: timing the market can be difficult, especially for young investors with insufficient knowledge of the market.

While professional day traders and some investors do employ chart analysis, economic forecasts, and even their intuition to predict the market, few can do it consistently. Market timing does not produce much higher returns than the buy-and-hold approach, which entails buying and holding equities for the long term.

Economists have a reputation for generating wildly erroneous forecasts. Despite in-depth statistics and fancy computer models and algorithms, economic forecasts are still inaccurate, according to a study conducted by the Federal Reserve in the United States.

Since the 2008 financial crisis, the gap between prognosis and reality appears to be expanding. This incredible discovery has far-reaching ramifications. The bottom line is that the market is impossible to anticipate all of the time.

So, if you hear about a successful market timing example, it could be due to luck rather than logic. According to the widely recognized research of "Determinants of Portfolio Performance", asset allocation decisions, rather than market timing, offer a better explanation for portfolio performance.

It is difficult to time the market, and ensuring sure your portfolio is correctly allocated at the right time can be even more difficult.

LACK OF PATIENCE

Slow and steady wins the race, as they say. Many years of hard work and patience are required for success. There are not many examples of overnight success. People, in the vast majority of cases, confront numerous challenges and roadblocks in accomplishing their goals and dreams.

Investing, in particular, is not always easy. There will be times when you lose money or make a small profit. Successful investors, on the other hand, retain a level head rather than becoming flustered. In the face of adversity, they do not make rash decisions.

As a result, you should always have realistic expectations for your portfolio and take risks that you are comfortable with. If something seems too good to be true, it most likely is. If a company claims significant returns in a short period of time using a specific trading technique, be suspicious and conduct your homework because there could be a catch somewhere. Ask yourself, "Why isn't everyone doing it if the rewards are so great?" When presented with such claims, this should be the first notion that comes to mind.

Your portfolio will be able to generate a significant return over time if you make wise investing decisions.

TRYING TO BREAK EVEN ON LOSING STOCK

Unfortunately, even when the writing's on the wall, novice investors have a tendency for clinging to failing equities. In such situations, the best plan of action is to limit and cut your losses by selling sinking equities before they fall even worse.

Some investors, on the other hand, are holding such equities in the hopes of recouping their losses. Unfortunately, this will not only worsen their losses, but will also wipe out their profits (if any). Their reasoning is based on a concept known as "cognitive mistake" in behavioral finance.

This misconception will not only worsen losses and offset profits, but it will also result in opportunity costs or missed earnings because the money acquired by selling these falling equities could have been invested in more profitable stocks that would have yielded dividends and capital gains.

This behavior is similar to that found in gambling where gamblers try to make up for lost bets by placing more bets, but they just wind up aggravating their condition.

THE HERD MENTALITY

When a market slump occurs, many investors become frightened and sell their stock. This is known as "panic-selling".

Smart investors, on the other hand, do not mindlessly follow the herd. They understand that stock market downturns are common and that the best strategy is to "buy and hold" when the market fluctuates. For example, Bank of America Merrill Lynch discovered that buy-and-hold investors had outperformed panic sellers every decade since 1960.

In a slump, astute investors find possibilities. Some of the most successful investors have taken advantage of stock market crashes to purchase shares at rock-bottom prices, which have since proven to be extremely profitable. During an economic downturn, you may have to deal with low yields. When the situation returns to normal, though, you will get considerably better results. Based on stock performance in the past, the average yield will be around 10 percent.

To cut a long story short, stay away from the herd mentality. Stay cool and know that stock prices and yields will certainly rebound within 18 months, no matter how drastically the market varies. If you're having trouble controlling your emotions, there's a simple solution: set up automatic deposits to a bargain brokerage or a robo-advisor. You'll avoid the temptation to put off investing by making your donations automatic.

You won't have to worry about herd mentality or panic selling if you use a robo-advisor. Robo-advisors like Wealthsimple use computers to take the emotion out of investing and conduct logical trades at the proper times based on facts.

You might assume you're at a disadvantage here if you're utilizing an online brokerage because you've chosen to perform some DIY investing. That, however, is not the case. While self-directed online brokerages won't tell you which stocks to buy and sell, they will provide you with a wealth of materials to aid in your decision-making, such as research papers, news articles, and in-depth stock analysis. Questrade excels at this, and you can reach out to them for assistance with trade execution or resource discovery.

INVESTING BEFORE YOU ARE READY

First and foremost, never invest until you're ready both financially and mentally.

Before you begin investing, pay off your high-interest debt. If you're in debt and paying 18 percent interest per year (which isn't uncommon), any money you put into equities has to earn more than 18 percent just to keep you from losing ground. The stock market's annual returns have averaged around 10 percent, not 18 percent, throughout long periods of time with many periods showing significantly lower returns.

It's also a good idea to have a fully-stocked emergency fund before you start investing in stocks. Ideally, you should have six to twelve months' worth of living expenditures on hand. A costly car repair or unexpected medical bill can compel you to sell your stocks at a bad moment, such as when they've temporarily dipped in value, causing you to miss out on future gains if you don't have an emergency fund.

SETTING UNREALISTIC EXPECTATIONS

It feels nice to put your money to work, and investing can be thrilling. Many people who are just getting started in investing are seeking to get rich soon as a result of these mistakes.

There is always the possibility of making a lot of money rapidly, but you need to adopt a long-term and balanced perspective. Some tips to remember:

- Never invest money in stocks that you will need in the next five years because the stock market might fall and take years to recover.
- Have realistic expectations when it comes to stock market investing. For example, the market's long-term average yearly profit is nearly 10 percent, but it can spike by 25 percent or more in certain years and decline by 25 percent or more in others. Expect a lot of volatility and keep in mind that just a few stocks will provide long-term average returns of more than 20 percent.

TRUSTING THE WRONG PEOPLE OR RESOURCES

Many new investors place too much trust in financial TV talk show hosts or hot stock advice from a friend or co-worker. Anyone can recommend a stock, but you rarely know the recommender's track record. Not to mention that even the best investor will occasionally make a terrible decision.

Investors can also be deceived by cold callers who disturb an evening with a pressing pitch to put money into a one-of-a-kind, cannot-lose investment. For example, a company that is supposedly on the approach of curing a disease or striking gold or oil. Keep in mind, if something appears to be too good to be true, it most likely is.

EXPECTING PAST PERFORMANCE TO CONTINUE

If you are looking for stocks or mutual funds to invest in, it can be difficult to pass up those that have had a very successful year, possibly increasing by 60 percent or more or even expanding in value.

However, keep in mind that outstanding results do not often repeat themselves year after year, especially with mutual funds. It is possible that a rapidly developing company's stock will rise for several years in a row, but this is not guaranteed. And a high gain in a mutual fund could be an exception.

It is fine to wish for excellent results from your investments, but do not bank on them or expect you will get them every year.

NOT EVALUATING YOUR PERFORMANCE

When it comes to outperforming benchmarks, investors should evaluate their own performance on a regular basis. If they invest in individual equities, it makes sense to strive to outperform the S&P 500, especially since any of them could invest in a solid low-fee S&P 500 index fund. It will be wiser to keep money in the index fund if they do not do so over a period of years.

Do not give up after a single year (or maybe two) of underperformance. Instead, look back over a few years to see how well you have done. If you continue to read and learn about investing, you may be able to improve your tactics over time.

NOT KEEPING UP WITH YOUR INVESTMENT

Even if you aim to be a buy-and-hold investor, you should not forget about your stocks if you have a large number of them. Keep track of them for the best results in your investing at least quarterly for most.

Look up what management has said about the company's performance and strategy in their quarterly financial reports.

Then, as time passes, assess how well management has carried out its strategy.

Look up the company in the news to see what you can find out. You'll want to be aware of any major developments, such as new product releases or declining sales.

NOT REBALANCING YOUR PORTFOLIO

This issue frequently occurs without your knowledge. To begin, you purchase assets in the proportions that you desire for your portfolio. Perhaps you have 75 percent of your portfolio invested in equities and 25 percent in bonds.

However, five years later, your equities may have grown to account for 85 percent or 90 percent of your portfolio, which is more than you intended to keep. A rebalance of your portfolio is long overdue. To re-establish the stock-bond proportions you want, you'll need to sell some stocks and acquire more bonds.

Stocks are not the only thing that can go wrong. If you own fifteen different stocks and one of them has risen in value, it may now account for 20 percent of the total value of your portfolio. If that's the case, that's a lot of money for one stock, so you should sell part of those shares and disperse the proceeds.

Keep in mind, though, that tremendous wealth is typically produced by allowing great stocks to continue to grow, so stay invested with a significant amount as long as the firm is healthy and expanding and you have faith in it.

BUYING MORE OF A FALLEN STOCK

This may appear to be counterintuitive. It is true that when the stock market as a whole falls, it is a perfect time to buy shares of great companies. However, that is not to say that you should buy more of it.

Stocks frequently fall for a good cause. Investigate what is going on before buying any additional stocks. You might even decide that selling the stock is a good idea. Do not buy more stock until you're confident that the company's current difficulty, such as the departure of its CEO or a disappointing earnings report, is just temporary.

INVESTING WITH BORROWED MONEY

You may become enthralled by the notion of investing using borrowed funds, i.e., using "margin". It can be exciting, even. Assume you put $10,000 into a stock and it doubles in value to $15,000 after a 50 percent gain. Isn't it fantastic? But what if you took out a $10,000 loan and put $20,000 into the stock? Then you'd have $30,000 in your pocket.

Margin is entirely legal and can considerably increase your profits – but it can also greatly increase your losses. If the stock you borrowed money to buy drops 50 percent in value, your $20,000 investment will be worth $10,000 – the loan amount. You'll be left with $0 once you've paid it back, implying that your 50 percent loss has now become a 100 percent loss due to margin.

In addition, the equity in your account serves as collateral for the loan. If the value of your margined investments begins to decline dramatically, your broker will issue a "margin call", requesting that you sell certain assets to produce cash or deposit additional cash into your account. If you don't, the brokerage may sell part of your assets on your behalf.

Brokerages, on the other hand, charge you interest if you use margin. Recent rates at one large brokerage, for example, ranged from 8.075 percent for loans of $250,000 to $499,999 to 9.825 percent for loans of less than $25,000. To make the loan profitable, you'll need to achieve a high rate of return. For most investors, margin is best avoided.

NOT CONTINUING TO LEARN

The more you know, the less likely you are to make mistakes. Your reading and thinking may also lead to improved investing techniques and performance.

Learn about successful investors. Learn about successful firms. It is also a good idea to read about business failures because they may be quite educational. Learn about effective management styles because the most successful organizations will have excellent management. Learn about the difficulties, prospects, and which players are the strongest and weakest in industries that interest you.

In the end, there is always more to learn to better your investment opportunities and prepare for inevitable shifts in the marketplace.

NOT MAKING USE OF INDEX FUNDS

It takes a lot of effort to build a successful track record of picking terrific individual stocks and holding them for long periods of time. It necessitates a great deal of reading, studying, deliberation, and luck. Many of us don't have the time or aren't interested in doing all of that.

Investing in a low-cost, broad-market index fund, such as one based on the S&P 500, is the best option for most consumers. This will provide you nearly the same returns as the stock market as a whole.

PUTTING TOO MANY EGGS IN ONE BASKET

If you put all of your money into a few stocks, you will have less room for error if something goes wrong. Of course, there is a benefit to what you are doing: if you invest all of your money in one stock and it doubles, your portfolio doubles as well!

However, if the stock falls by 40 percent, your entire portfolio falls with it. Although there is no ideal number of stocks to purchase, having fewer than fifteen or so can put you at risk.

You shouldn't necessarily strive to buy fifty or over a hundred stocks, as this can lead to a situation where a single stock's performance has little impact on your whole portfolio. And the more you own, the more difficult it will be to keep track of each position.

Many people consider ten to twenty stocks to be a reasonable quantity.

EXPECTING NO RISK WHEN DIVERSIFIED

Even if you have someone to assist you and/or your portfolio is well-diversified, do not expect to have zero risks when it comes to investing. There will always be ups and downs in the stock market, real estate prices, and other financial markets no matter how good your portfolio and judgments are.

You must be aware that there is always the possibility of losing money, experiencing downtimes, or experiencing volatile markets (like stock corrections or bear markets). You can escape the "selling low, buying high" trap by accepting it, keeping to your plan, and staying focused on long-term financial goals.

When markets are falling and the news is full of doom and gloom, it's natural to feel anxious. You'll be alright if you train yourself to block out the noise and keep investing. There are moments when you should be more cautious and leave some money on the sidelines, but for the most part, you should keep your positions and keep going.

YOU HAVE NO IDEA WHY YOU ARE INVESTING

If you do not know why you want to invest your money or why you are already doing so, you may be setting yourself up for failure. This is because, if you do not know, it is likely that you do not care either. Make some financial goals for yourself, both now and in the future.

Is your goal to accumulate assets for the future, expedite your retirement, generate passive income through dividends, and retire early? Then you must have a strategy in place.

What assets will help you achieve your objectives, how much can you afford to risk right now, and what and where are you investing?

Those objectives and your strategy may alter over time, which is entirely okay. The goal is to keep you on track, involved in your investments, and more prepared in your decisions.

EXCESSIVE FOCUS ON THE NEWS

The foreign exchange market is heavily influenced by news with traders reacting to economic reports, central bank commentary, and broader political happenings. Traders who are just starting out should remember that the market's interpretation of the news is all that matters and their own opinions have no bearing on market dynamics.

For example, a trader may believe that solid Eurozone economic statistics should be bullish for EUR/USD, but the market may disagree on any given day. Traders should constantly focus on the market rather than their personal interpretation of the news flow since failing to respect the market's opinion will result in a loss.

IGNORING THE NEWS

While paying too much attention to the news is likely to harm your performance, avoiding the news is not an option. Because such news is frequently market-moving, you should always be aware of significant economic reports and their release dates.

PENNY STOCKS HAVE GOTTEN THE BETTER OF INVESTORS

One of the most common mistakes that new investors make is being drawn in by chances that look to be easy money, such as penny stock opportunities. Despite the fact that it looks to be a brilliant concept, in which you can buy a huge number of shares for a small sum of money, it is not.

Doing anything is not a good idea. One of the problems with penny stocks is that, while some people can profit from them, the industry is filled with con artists, making it impossible to trust anyone. They are well aware that new investors are about to enter the market and will be unfamiliar with penny stocks and how to invest in them correctly.

As a result, these charlatans prey on naive investors by making it appear as if penny stocks might make you a lot more money than they actually can.

Because the stocks are so cheap, it is typical for dishonest people to buy huge quantities of them in order to raise the stock's price. When the price of anything is a dollar or at most five dollars a share, this is not difficult to achieve. After that, they might keep track of the price increase in a product they are selling, such as an online video course on penny stocks or one of the many newsletters that circulate (usually online).

This form of publishing is easily influenced by those looking for quick cash or are ordinary people with genuine needs and good intentions, but are unaware of the specifics of the situation.

It is strongly advised that you fight the urge to give in and follow the crowd. If you want to be an investor, you do not need to consider penny stocks at all. At some point in the future, one in a thousand will prove to be a viable enterprise.

Choosing that one in a thousand, on the other hand, is a futile exercise. It is highly improbable that a new investor will pick the winning penny stock and this is especially true if you are a newbie investor.

Also, remember that just because something is pricey upfront does not mean it is a fantastic deal. As a result, buying a one-dollar stock could be as profitable as throwing money in the fire.

CONCLUSION

In brief, you may invest your money for the future in a variety of ways, but it always boils down to common sense and thorough research. Never make a hasty decision and always double-check if the investment is worthwhile.

Regardless, it is important to begin investing in your future as soon as possible. Many people miss out on substantial chances because they do not seize every opportunity that comes their way, and the stock market is an excellent area to gain money. However, in order to achieve the greatest potential results, you must first educate yourself.

There is a good chance you will make a lot of money if you invest in stocks or trade in the stock market. However, when it comes to stock investments, caution is required. As an investor, you must have a thorough understanding of stocks and how they are exchanged in the market.

If you read this book thoroughly, you will be aware of some of the benefits of investing early that are summarized below:

You will have a larger selection of investment tools since you will have more time to invest and learn more about how to make money through investing.

The reason for this is simple: when you are in your 30s or 40s, you will be focused on saving for retirement, your children's education, or other ambitions such as buying a house or a car, making it much more difficult to learn about investing and thus save enough money for those goals.

It will help you get a leg up on the competition in our global financial system.

Many millionaires are simply those who began investing early. This is especially true in China where many poor families struggle to pay for their children's education. If you become wealthy earlier, it will be much easier to send your children abroad to study or to attend an expensive private school.

It will enable you to make significant investments.

It will be much easier for you to make substantial stock and real estate investments if you are a young man or woman who is already making decent money. There's no denying that investing $10,000 all at once is a lot easier than saving up the same amount of money while still paying bills.

After investing, accumulating wealth will be easy for you.

When you are in your teens or twenties, you have many years ahead of you to continue investing, so even if your rate of return is only 10 percent, it can still add up to a significant amount when invested year after year.

It will assist you in forming a network of affluent friends who will be able to assist you in obtaining additional possibilities in life.

You might have a friend who already owns a profitable firm or is a successful businessman; if so, this will considerably increase your chances of landing a position that pays well.

In conclusion, this book provides you with all of the tools you need to invest in the stock market and answer many of the questions you may have. Your trading adventure is about to start.

Please consider leaving a review on Amazon if you enjoyed this book so that others might enjoy it as well.

REFERENCES

Benson, Alana. "Investment Portfolio." Nerdwallet. May 18, 2021. https://www.nerdwallet.com/article/investing/investment-portfolio

Business Standard. "What is IPO." Business Standard. Aug 23, 2021. https://www.business-standard.com/about/what-is-ipo#collapse

Economic Times. "Stock Market Terms for Beginners." India Times. Aug 24, 2021. https://economictimes.indiatimes.com125-stock-market-terms-for-beginners/tomorrowmakersshow/70188991.cms

Fernando, Jason. "Compound Interest." Investopedia. Feb 16, 2021. https://www.investopedia.com/terms/c/compoundinterest.aspx

Fidelity. "What is an IRA?" Fidelity. Aug 25, 2021. https://www.fidelity.com/building-savings/learn-about-iras/what-is-an-ira

Folger, Ean. "Advantages of Investing In Your 20s." Investopedia. Jan 10, 2021. https://www.investopedia.com/financial-edge/0212/5-advantages-to-investing-in-your-20s.aspx

Goldman, Andrew. "Best Investment Options in Canada." Wealthsimple. April 21, 2021. https://www.wealthsimples.com/en-ca/learn/best-investment-options#2

Gomez, Osvaldo. *Stock Market Investing for Minority Teens & Friends: What it takes to learn and master the Wall Street hustle.* Self-Published. Jan 27, 2020.

Hayes, Adam. "Liquidity." Investopedia. Aug 20, 2021. https://www.investopedia.com/terms/l/liquidity.asp

James, Robert. *Stock Market Investing for Beginners: Understanding the basics of how to make money with stocks.* JNR via PublishDrive. July 9, 2021.

Kasasa. "Beginners Guide to Understanding 401k Plans." Kasasa. May 14, 2021. https://www.kasasa.com/blog/401k-guide/

Muller, Chris. "Why You Should Start Investing Early as Possible." Young and Thrifty. May 19, 2020. https://youngandthrifty.ca/why-investing-early-as-possible

O'Shea, Arielle. "Different Types of Stocks You Should Know." Nerdwallet. Aug 18, 2021. https://www.nerdwallet.com/ article/investing/types-of-stocks

Reed, Eric. "Short Term vs. Long Term Investing." The Street. Feb 19, 2020. https://www.thestreet.com/investing/short-term-investing-vs-long-term-investing

Reinkensmeyer, Blain. "Best Canadian Brokers for Stock Trading." Stockbrokers. Aug 26, 2021. https://www.stockbrokers. com/guides/best-brokers-canada

Revenue Agency. "Registered Retirement Savings Plan." Canada. Jan 7, 2021. https://www.canada.ca/en/revenue-agency/services/tax/individuals/topics/rrsps-related-plans/ registered-retirement-savings-plan-rrsp.html/

Taylor, Ben. "How to Pick Your Investment." Investopedia. Jun 15, 2021. https://www.investopedia.com/investing/how-pick-your-investments/

Town, Phil. "50 Warren Buffet Quote on Investing." Life and Success. Aug 21, 2021. https://www.ruleoneinvesting.com/ blog/how-to-invest/warren-buffett-quotes-on-investing-success/

Volgt, Kevin. "Best Online Brokers for Stock Trading." Nerdwallet. Aug 19, 2021. https://www.nerdwallet.com/best/ investing/online-brokers-for-stock-trading

Made in United States
Troutdale, OR
12/18/2024

26838254R00096